James Lynn Greenstone, EdD, JD, DABECI

The Elements of Police Hostage and Crisis Negotiations
Critical Incidents and How to Respond to Them

*Pre-publication
REVIEWS,
COMMENTARIES,
EVALUATIONS . . .*

"This is more than a good book—it is a great plan! Experts in this field always agree that the successful resolution to every police hostage or crisis negotiation begins with a plan. Entering this endeavor without a plan is like sailing the sea sans navigational equipment.

Dr. Jim Greenstone boils it down to the basics with the same succinctness he used in *Elements of Crisis Intervention* and *Elements of Mediation*. Drawing from a wealth of real world experience he winnowed this work through his police heart, psychologist's psyche, and lawyer's preciseness to weave a seamless set of extensive, eclectic, and exceptional principles for perusal by all professionals in the police world.

Here is some advice from an 'old guy' on the job to my brothers-and-sisters-in-arms. Read this, reckon with it, secure it in your ready bags. Without doubt, you will return and rely on it."

Rod Fowler, EdD, PhD, DABECI
*Professor Emeritus,
University of Tennessee at Chattanooga;
Chattanooga Police Department
SWAT and HNT (Retired)*

More pre-publication
REVIEWS, COMMENTARIES, EVALUATIONS . . .

"This body of work brings together the academic principles with the empirically learned operational procedures of hostage recovery and crisis intervention. Dr. Greenstone points out the possible pitfalls of both the psychological elements and the legal constraints, using case law. The concept of starting with a 'Directory' to steer readers/practitioners to their specific questions is unique and effective. He follows through with the appropriate use of checklists, worksheets, and scales. Finally, the Hostage Negotiator's Training Laboratory developed by Dr. Greenstone will be invaluable in establishing the benchmark for training in this millennium."

Detective Captain Frank A. Bolz Jr., AAS, BS, N.Y.P.D. (Retired)
Founder of the NYPD Hostage Negotiating Program;
Chief Negotiator, 1973-1982

The Haworth Press®
New York • London • Oxford

The Elements
of Police Hostage
and Crisis Negotiations
Critical Incidents
and How to Respond to Them

THE HAWORTH PRESS
Hostage and Crisis Negotiation
James Greenstone, EdD
Senior Editor

The Elements of Police Hostage and Crisis Negotiations: Critical Incidents and How to Respond to Them by James Lynn Greenstone

Other Titles of Related Interest

A Handbook for Psychological Fitness-for-Duty Evaluations in Law Enforcement by Cary D. Rostow and Robert D. Davis

Risky Business: Managing Employee Violence in the Workplace by Lynne Falkin McClure

Threats in Schools: A Practical Guide for Managing Violence by Joseph T. McCann

Threat Assessment: A Risk Management Approach by James T. Turner and Michael G. Gelles

Terrorism: Strategies for Intervention edited by Harold V. Hall

The Elements
of Police Hostage
and Crisis Negotiations
Critical Incidents
and How to Respond to Them

James Lynn Greenstone, EdD, JD, DABECI

The Haworth Press®
New York • London • Oxford

The Haworth Press, Inc., 10 Alice Street, Binghamton, NY 13904-1580.

"Thoughts on Negotiation," copyright 1992 by Tony Arnold, is reprinted by permission.

Chapter 5 was originally published as part of "Psychopathy and Hostage Negotiations: Some Preliminary Thoughts and Findings" in Carl Gacano (Ed.), *The Clinical and Forensic Assessment of Psychopathy: A Practitioner's Guide* (pp. 385-391), by Lawrence Erlbaum Associates, copyright 2000.

AUTHOR'S NOTE
The information contained in this book is not intended for general use or for public consumption. It is intended for use by sworn police hostage and crisis negotiators, for police tactical officers, for police commanders, for assigned police psychologists, and for those others assigned to work in this specialized area, on a need-to-know basis. Please control the dissemination of this information accordingly.

Cover design by Lora Wiggins.

Library of Congress Cataloging-in-Publication Data

Greenstone, James L.
    The elements of police hostage and crisis negotiations : critical incidents and how to respond to them / James Lynn Greenstone.
        p. cm.
    "Not intended for general use or for public consumption."
    Includes bibliographical references and index.
    ISBN 0-7890-1895-0 (hard : alk. paper)—ISBN 0-7890-1896-9 (soft : alk. paper)
    1. Hostages. 2. Hostage negotiations. 3. Police training. 4. Communication in law enforcement.
I. Title.
HV8058.G74 2004
363.2'3—dc22
                                                                                        2004004258

"When people need help, they call the police. When the police need help, they call SWAT and the hostage negotiation team. When SWAT and the hostage negotiation team need help, they call Dr. Fowler."

With this quote from those who know his illustrious career, this book is dedicated to Dr. W. Rodney Fowler. He is the consummate professional, a teacher and a distinguished professor, a police officer and a real friend from whom I have learned for many years. In this specific context, he is a pioneer in the field of crisis intervention and police hostage negotiation. When his department needed someone to talk a person off the top of a bridge or out of a secure stronghold, the first call was placed to Dr. Fowler.

I first met Dr. Fowler when he reached out to a crisis victim, in an unusual situation, when all other interveners held back and failed to offer the needed assistance. Throughout our friendship and our professional association, he has always been there to offer the very best that he had.

When looking for the right person to whom this book should be dedicated, no one else that I know better exemplifies all for which the police negotiator stands, and for all that the police negotiator does, than Dr. Fowler. This book is honored by him, and I thank him for all that he has given to me and to our shared discipline.

ABOUT THE AUTHOR

James L. Greenstone, EdD, JD, DABECI, is a Police Mental Health Consultant and Deputy Sheriff with the Tarrant County Sheriff's Department in Fort Worth, Texas. He has served as Director of the Psychological Services Unit of the Fort Worth Police Department in Texas, where he supervised the department's Peer Support Team, was Coordinator of the Critical Incident Stress Management Program, and was a member of the department's Hostage and Crisis Negotiations Team. He has been in practice for 37 years and has been a police officer for 25 years. Previously, he served with the Dallas County Sheriff's Department and with the Lancaster, Texas, Police Department. He is certified as a Master Peace Officer and as a Mental Health Peace Officer by the Texas Commission on Law Enforcement Officer Standards and Education. He holds police instructor certificates from Texas and several other states.

Dr. Greenstone is Editor of the *Journal of Police Crisis Negotiations* (Haworth), has edited the *Journal of Crisis Negotiations* and *The International Journal of Police Negotiations and Crisis Management,* and was Editor-in-Chief of *Emotional First Aid: A Journal of Crisis Intervention.* He has been an Adjunct Professor of Law at the Texas Wesleyan University School of Law and was Lead Hostage and Crisis Negotiations Instructor at the North Central Texas Council of Governments Regional Police Academy.

CONTENTS

Foreword

This work represents an extraordinary, most useful endeavor by an acknowledged, active authority in the field of police hostage and crisis negotiations. It is much more than a book. It is a carefully crafted set of tools specially designed to assist those undertaking this arduous, intellectually taxing duty. Negotiation is a proven instrument, indeed, the preferred instrument for the resolution of conflict of all kinds, in which the police authority is necessarily involved. Although this work is based, substantially, on the experience gained through the evolution and study of the phenomenon of hostage-taking responses in the United States, the principles set out are of universal validity and application. They are thus deserving of the closest examination by police authorities everywhere, that this learning may be adapted and adopted wherever life may be in danger as a result of this kind of criminal behavior.

Hostage taking, in all its various forms, is not something new. It has probably been around since the dawn of mankind in some sort of society. Over the millennia, it has evoked all types of responses, all too many of them resulting in enhanced social bitterness and loss of human life. Over the past thirty or so years a more helpful and responsible attitude toward these matters has developed within the United States law enforcement community, encouraged by a perceptive, socially conscious judiciary. Negotiation has become more than the preferred way of handling these distressing events, whatever might have occasioned them. It is now a matter of settled law. It is, therefore, incumbent upon all police authorities throughout the United States to acquaint their personnel, at all levels, with their responsibilities in this regard and to prepare, adequately, specialists to undertake the tasks of putting into practice all that is comprehended by the term "negotiation" as may be required in the instant case. This is, indeed, a heavy responsibility, with awesome consequences. It is perilous to neglect it in any particular.

Dr. Greenstone's work is expressly designed to assist those in whom these obligations legally and morally reside. While resting upon a substantial body of both theory and practice, it is beyond both. It is very much a "how-to" text for instructors and practitioners occupying a variety of roles. It is, therefore, a work of singular utility, much needed, and to be welcomed as a worthy effort by one so qualified by experience and enthusiasm to undertake its synthesis.

Police crisis and hostage negotiation, as it has evolved, has been the product of a fine, multidisciplinary approach. It is quite extraordinary how the various approaches have melded, seamlessly, into a cohesive whole. There has been a commendable lack of hubris informing these efforts. Yet a great deal of what is now taken for granted was once the subject of much soul-searching and heated debate. Negotiation, as a technique in this field of endeavor, had many competitors and a good deal of philosophical opposition. The present work stands clearly above the fray. It is designed to take the best experience of all the relevant disciplines and to reduce it to easily understood and communicated basics that might, most expeditiously, achieve the optimum results. It is, in the first instance, an excellent teaching tool developed and refined at the hands of an academically qualified, law enforcement instructor. Its systematic presentation constitutes, of itself, an excellent lesson plan for training at all levels and for all roles. A sure welcome is to be found for this book in the libraries of all police training academies, however grand or humble. For those whose duties must, perforce, include a substantial amount of on-the-job training, the individual possession of this book will constitute an invaluable source of consultation under all conditions. Its arrangement and patent simplicity are intended to facilitate reference during even the most tense, operational moments. Hopefully, at some future date, it may acquire much the same utility as *Robert's Rules of Order,* so that police crisis and hostage negotiations will say, in the most practical of circumstances, "What does Greenstone have to say about this?"

The literature on this subject area is now most extensive, though one would not gather that impression by reading some of the annexed bibliographies. This book entertains no unrealistic ambitions to supplement any of this material; it acknowledges it appropriately and moves to supplement it. In truth, it is really quite different from anything previously published elsewhere in its purpose, content, and methodology. Its success will depend very much on its adoption and implementation as a training and operational adjunct. Careful study of this text should convince those to whom it is directed of its usefulness in promoting improved performance and success, generally, in the matter of conflict resolution. The key to such success is in the field of training and, here, it may be averred with confidence, this text will have no rivals. Dr. Greenstone has done a great service to the law enforcement community in applying himself to producing this work. He will surely be gratified in the years to come in witnessing how his labors contribute to the dissemination of these basic elements to all who might benefit from a more perfect knowledge of them and their application to their vitally important work.

H. H. A. Cooper
Professor, School of General Studies
The University of Texas at Dallas

Preface

The elements, or the basics, of any discipline are critical to achieving success. *The Elements of Police Hostage and Crisis Negotiations* focuses on those basics that are needed by police negotiators in the field. The presentation is ordered in such a way as to provide quick and easy access to the information needed from the initial callout to the final debriefing. Tables of contents were developed that respond to specific needs. The main table of contents is prescriptive in nature so that it can be used as a self-contained guide to negotiations. Other tables help guide users to specific types of crises or to procedures and techniques. These tables guide the user to the chapters of the book that are related. These chapters contain more useful checklists and procedural notes that are related to the negotiations process. The entire work is designed to be user-friendly and to provide field negotiators with what they need when they need it. This is done without the theory that often accompanies. Those who want theoretical depth are guided to other sources that can provide such information. This is an uncomplicated book that reflects what is known in this field and then funnels it to the intervener.

Although there are few extensive works in the field of hostage negotiations, *The Elements of Police Hostage and Crisis Negotiations* can serve as a companion text in the field, or stand by itself in the negotiator's gearbag. It is what is needed to get the job done, and nothing more. The lists, procedures, suggestions, and guidelines are field-tested and directly related to field situations. Because no two situations are the same, allowance is made for such differences and additional suggestions are offered for making the necessary adjustments.

The practice of police hostage and crisis negotiations has been reduced to its basic elements so that they can be applied as broadly as possible, and are presented in a format that is useful both for the experienced professional and for the novice. I know of no other text that approaches the subject so directly. Much time has been spent eliminating confusion about procedures and about how to deal with crises.

This book reinforces the theoretical framework that postulates police hostage negotiations as a viable discipline in its own right.

Because this is a practical guide, most theory purposely has been omitted. It is suggested that *The Elements of Police Hostage and Crisis Negotiations* be used as a supplement in related criminal justice, crisis intervention, and psychology classes. This work is also appropriate for training courses in hostage and crisis negotiations and first response to hostage and barricaded situations. The experienced negotiator can use this book independently in the field, in training, and in the office.

This book is designed to aid in practical, day-to-day, on-the-scene hostage and crisis negotiations by all law enforcement officers. In addition to listing the areas covered in the chapters, the table of contents is a *step-by-step guide* to the intervention and negotiations process. It should be used by negotiators to guide an intervention in an orderly fashion. For the experienced negotiator, the table of contents is a helpful reminder of the steps to be taken during a hostage or barricaded situation. Novices may need to read the entire book carefully before they can use the table of contents effectively. They should understand that the full value of this book depends on their gaining theoretical depth and practical training. Negotiators can also look up material according to the activity they want to perform or by the negotiator's role (e.g., primary negotiator, coach, intelligence coordinator, or police psychologist). These listings are printed on the inside front and back covers of the book for added convenience in field conditions.

Acknowledgments

This work is a compilation of material that has been gathered from police negotiators around the world with whom I have been privileged to work and to train. They have been my teachers as much as I have been theirs.

Of particular note are the following:

Dr. Sharon C. Leviton for her constant and consistent love, input, and encouragement.

Dr. Edward S. Rosenbluh for being my mentor and critic for almost forty years. I would tell him my opinion, and he would tell me why I was wrong.

Dr. W. Rodney Fowler for his guidance and direction.

Dr. H. H. A. "Tony" Cooper for his foreword to this book, and for his friendship and encouragement.

Lieutenant Roger Dixon for always being honest with me when we were in the field.

Ms. Suzanne Raif for her organization and administrative skills, and for typing much of this material.

Dr. Mike McMains for his collegial support and encouragement.

Constable Tony Arnold for his direct contribution of his poem to this book and to all negotiators who stand and talk.

Lieutenant Jim Oney for being my role model of a police officer.

Grand Master Richard Morris for raising the bar in the martial arts and for raising the bar for me specifically. What I learned from him about the soul of a warrior translates directly into the special task of hostage and crisis negotiations.

Bill Palmer, Vice President and Publications Director, The Haworth Press, Inc., for his encouragement.

Kathy Rutz, Vice President, Special Projects, The Haworth Press, Inc., for her friendship, assistance, and love of pumpkins.

And Captain Frank A. Bolz Jr., who started it all.

Therefore but a single person was created in the world, to teach that if any man has caused a single life to perish from Israel, he is deemed by Scripture as if he had caused a whole world to perish; and anyone who saves a single soul from Israel, he is deemed by Scripture as if he had saved a whole world.

From the Talmud, Sanhedrin,
Chapter four, Mishnah five, Section three

"Thoughts on Negotiation"

You stand and talk to doors and walls
No response . . . no one calls.
Frustration's seen but never heard,
All of this, seems so absurd.
A voice, a cry, contact at last;
Adrenalin flows so very fast.
Keep it boring, keep it calm
No one must come to any harm.
Violent tones, all aimed at you,
Don't let your feelings show through.
Criminal, terrorist, or just mad,
Whoever thought it would be so bad.
Think intel first, second, and last,
But take care not to probe too fast.
Some commanders command, others do not;
Yet another unknown to affect the plot.
Demands appear at the drop of a hat,
Remember, remember don't call them that.
A deadline's here, talk it through,
Before they really turn the screw.
The victim sounds so terrified,
Offer hope, stay by her side.
So it goes, on and on,
Until it ends, until it's done.
If it all ends fine, it all goes well,
You really feel pretty swell.
If, however, the opposite's the case,
Who's to blame . . . the human race?
Was it all a dream, a mime?
A final thought . . . what about next time?

Constable/Negotiator Tony Arnold
Hendon, England, 1992
National Negotiator's School

Chapter 1

Preincident Preparation

SELECT NEGOTIATORS

Initial selection of negotiators can be done in more ways than are provided here. The importance of selection can be found in the procedures that are used to ensure that those who can function most effectively as negotiators are selected. How this is accomplished may vary from team to team, but remains at the core of the process. Random selection of negotiators cannot hope to provide the same level of excellence and psychological readiness as a well-developed procedure. In addition, well-defined procedures may serve to increase the credibility of the team in the eyes of other officers. Current negotiations team members can and should be involved in the selection process. Because all members of a negotiations team must work together very closely, unanimity among current members is important when deciding on new team members.

ESTABLISH SELECTION TIMELINE

Appropriate time should be allowed for each of these steps that are used by a specific team. More time will be needed for certain steps, while less will be needed for others. The first step for any team contemplating selecting team members is to decide what specific steps they want, or need, to use to accomplish their goal. Remember that the goal of a selection procedure is to acquire for the team the best negotiator candidates that are available.

Suggested Timeline and Selection Procedures

1. Write letter of interest and intent. Post the position appropriately according to departmental directives and policies. Ask that those interested reply by a certain date by letter or memo.

2. Review of applicant's letter by the hostage negotiations team. You may find it helpful to have a letter from the candidate's immediate supervisor, also. This will tell you more about the candidate, and it will also tell you if the immediate supervisor will support his or her activity on the team if selected.

3. Hostage negotiations team interviews. Those whose letters were found to be acceptable should be invited for individual interviews by members of the team.

4. Hostage negotiations team votes on continuing with candidate. After the interview, decide with which candidates the team would like to continue in the selection process. A unanimous vote of the team is better than a majority vote. All team members must work together closely.

5. Psychological testing is done. Consult with your police psychologist. Also, see what other teams in your area are doing in this regard. Although selection can be done effectively without this step, psychological testing provides an important dimension that may not become apparent to the team except after much involvement with the selected individuals. Psychological testing by someone familiar with using tests for this purpose will save you much time in the long run.

6. Assess the candidates. Put each continued candidate through an actual negotiations situation. Face-to-face or on the telephone will work nicely. Although the team should not expect the candidates to know all about negotiations, their reaction to the simulation will tell you much about how they might function once trained. Be sure that the actors put the candidates under a reasonable amount of stress in order to monitor their reactions.

7. Team holds final acceptance vote. Unanimity seems to work best, since everyone has to work with this person at some time and in some circumstances.

8. Approval by SWAT commander, chief of police, and others in administration as needed. This will vary from department to department. Check your policies.

9. Welcome ceremony for new negotiator(s). In conjunction with monthly meeting or training days? A formal welcome of some kind is good for team morale, and good for the sense of team identity that must be fostered in the selectee.
10. Issue gear to new negotiator. Award negotiator bar. Do this soon so that the new negotiator will be ready. Be sure to set the selected individual up for formal hostage and crisis negotiations training as the need dictates.

USE THE DECISION TREE

Based on these selection procedures, our decision tree may help in getting through the process. See Figure 1.1.

DEVELOP GENERAL ORDERS AND STANDING OPERATING PROCEDURES

The following are offered as examples of departmental general orders (GOs) and standing operating procedures (SOPs) for hostage and crisis negotiations operations. In most cases, general orders should be concise and limited. On the other hand, SOPs can be utilized to provide the specific details for such operations. GOs and SOPs should not be regarded as synonymous. Each has a purpose and these should not be confused.

Example of General Orders

TO: Chief of Police
FROM:
DATE:
SUBJECT: General Orders: Hostage and Crisis Negotiations Team Policy and Procedure

The primary goal in a hostage situation is to preserve the lives of all of those involved.

1. In all hostage situations, the ranking officer or supervisor on the scene shall be in command. This shall be the only person who can authorize the discharge of weapons except in emergency, self-defense situations.
2. The officer in charge shall immediately establish communications with others at the scene and with the dispatcher.

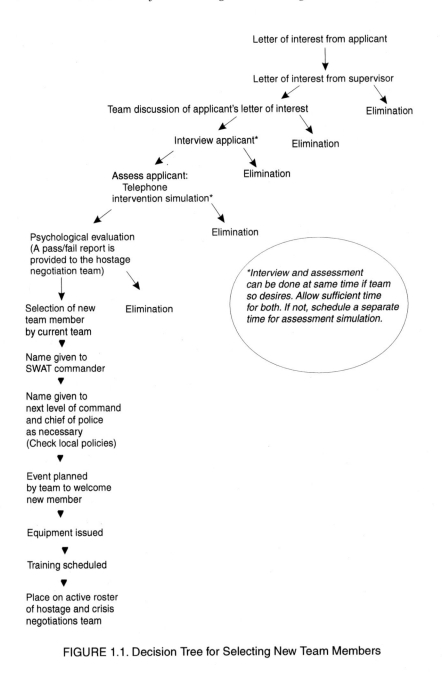

FIGURE 1.1. Decision Tree for Selecting New Team Members

3. The captain of the affected division shall be required to respond to any hostage situation.
4. Negotiators will not be commanders or in ultimate decision-making positions. Commanders and ultimate decision makers will not be negotiators.
5. A public information officer will be used to interact directly with the media after consultation with the incident commander.
6. The hostage negotiations team will be activated at the same time as the SWAT section is activated unless deemed inappropriate. Notification procedures for the hostage negotiations team will be the same as the notification procedure for the SWAT section. The hostage negotiations team and/or individual members of the hostage negotiations team will not be activated without activation of the SWAT section unless the situation requires only negotiators without the need for SWAT. The initial officer in charge at the scene of a hostage or barricaded incident prior to the arrival of the SWAT section and the hostage negotiations team shall use all reasonable means to establish a perimeter, stabilize the situation, and cause the SWAT section to be notified immediately.
7. Access will be restricted during hostage incidents to both the command post and to the hostage negotiations center. Guards will be posted, as necessary, to ensure compliance.
8. Deadlines will not be imposed on the hostage negotiations team by the on-scene commander, the Chief, or the "decision maker."

During mobile hostage situations, the following guidelines will be utilized:

1. The ranking patrol supervisor on the scene shall be in full command until properly relieved.
2. The ranking supervisor at the appropriate field operations division office shall be responsible for coordinating field and headquarters police activities.
3. The ranking supervisor in command at the scene shall be responsible for deciding if barricades shall be used and shall ensure that only the minimum number of patrol units required for this type of call are dispatched.
4. No other units are to be dispatched without approval from the person in command in the appropriate field operations division office. Specialized operations, such as air support, shall be utilized at the discretion of these persons.
5. If jurisdictions change during the course of this action, only the authorized number of patrol units may participate.
6. Once the mobile hostage situation becomes stationary, officers will secure the perimeter, and negotiators will attempt to negotiate the release of hostages.

Example of Standing Operating Procedures

TO: Chief of Police
FROM:
DATE:
SUBJECT: Hostage and Crisis Negotiations Team, Proposed Standing Operating Procedures

INTRODUCTION

The hostage and crisis negotiations team is established and trained to function during hostage situations, barricaded subjects, and/or with suicidal persons. The tactical goal of the team is the safety of all persons associated with the specific incident. These include the hostage taker, the barricaded subject, the hostage negotiators, all tactical personnel, the hostages, and any other police or civilians in the immediate area. This specific goal is to be met through intensive training of the hostage negotiations team in negotiation procedures and related techniques. All members of the team will be trained to function in all key positions related to hostage negotiations and support.

DEFINITIONS

hostage situation: Person(s) who has secreted himself or herself, and possibly others, in an inaccessible place and threatening to do bodily harm to himself or herself or to others or to destroy property. Some elements that characterize a hostage situation are as follows:

- Hostages held by the hostage taker
- Containment with threat of force by authorities
- Substantive demands by the hostage taker
- Communication between hostage taker and authorities
- A leader among hostage takers
- A negotiator for authorities
- Time
- A need to live on the part of the hostage taker

barricaded person: A barricaded person situation may present some of the same characteristics as in a hostage situation minus the hostages and will be treated as a crisis situation in order to assure the safety of all concerned.
barricaded sniper: A sharpshooter concealed to harass by picking off individuals, usually at long range, and with a telescope (sight-equipped rifle). A sniper, for purposes of this order, will be considered a barricaded person. A sniper situation is primarily a tactical response scenario if the sniper is endangering the lives of other people by shooting randomly and continuously.

Policy

1. Commanders and ultimate decision makers will not be negotiators.
2. A public information officer will be used to interact directly with the media after consultation with the incident commander.
3. General procedure will be to contain and isolate the subject, evaluate the situation, and negotiate as long as practical to assure a safe outcome for all concerned.
4. Barricaded subjects will be negotiated and handled as crisis victims to the fullest possible extent.
5. Only properly trained police personnel will be used as negotiators.
6. Police officers who may be taken hostage will be treated in the same manner as all other hostages regarding negotiations, surrender, and debriefing.
7. Negotiations will be instituted at the point that it is clear that a hostage situation is in progress, and will continue until the incident is resolved. Deaths surrounding the incident occurring prior to the beginning of negotiations will generally not be sufficient indication for tactical intervention. Generally, deaths occurring after the advent of negotiations will provide sufficient indication for tactical intervention. Such a decision is not made by the hostage negotiations team or tactical commander but by the incident commander.
8. The hostage negotiations team will be activated at the same time as the SWAT section is activated unless deemed inappropriate, or unless it is deemed appropriate to activate only the negotiations team. Notification procedures for the hostage negotiations team will be the same as the notification procedure for the SWAT section.
9. Face-to-face negotiations will not be considered in most instances unless deemed tactically necessary by the hostage negotiations team supervisor with concurrence of the SWAT commander and incident commander.
10. All surrenders will be coordinated between the hostage negotiations team and the SWAT section.

11. The hostage negotiations team will debrief all situations, regardless of outcome, either immediately after resolution of the incident or at a time and date designated by the hostage negotiations team supervisor.
12. All hostages released during or after the hostage incident will be debriefed immediately by members of the hostage negotiations team for the purpose of (1) attending to their emotional needs, and (2) gathering additional intelligence.
13. The following are generally negotiable items:

    - Food
    - Beverages
    - Media coverage
    - Help related to hostage taker's problems

14. The following are generally considered nonnegotiable items:

    - Weapons
    - Exchange of hostages for other hostages
    - Exchange of police officers for hostages
    - Drugs
    - Transportation
    - Freedom
    - Currency
    - Choice of negotiators

15. Discontinuation of all utilities, including telephone, used by the hostage taker will be considered only after all SWAT personnel are in position and the negotiations team has become operational. This provides for the possibility of uninterrupted contact with the hostage taker by use of a secured line in the case of the telephone, and for additional items to be negotiated in the case of the utilities.
16. Emergency medical services, fire service, and all related emergency services will be contacted in accordance with the general orders.
17. Anything given to the hostage taker usually will be given only in return for something of value given by him or her. Such give and take is necessary for the continuation of successful negotiations. Exceptions can be made at the discretion of the hostage negotiations team supervisor with concurrence of the

incident commander. Nonhostage crisis situations will not fall under this rule.

18. Access will be restricted during hostage incidents to both the command post and to the hostage negotiations center. Guards will be posted, as necessary, to ensure compliance.
19. Tactical use of the negotiator will be considered and accomplished as necessary for the satisfactory resolution of the incident.
20. Rank or titles of the negotiators will not be used during negotiations.
21. Time will be regarded and used to the advantage of the negotiator.
22. Once it has been established, by whatever means, that the hostages are safe, only minimal attention will be given to them until their release.
23. Generally, members of the hostage negotiations team will not encourage hostages to attempt escape.
24. Incident logs will be maintained on all situations.
25. Selection of the primary and secondary negotiator in a particular incident will be accomplished by the hostage negotiations team supervisor after considering all of the attendant factors:

    • Who is on the scene
    • Who is likely to arrive on the scene
    • Who is available
    • Who made initial contact
    • Who would be most effective under this particular circumstance
    • The desires of the on-scene commander when considered with all other factors
    • Time

26. The hostage negotiations team will receive a minimum of 100 hours training per year to include the following:

    • Forty hours formal classroom training (statutory requirement)
    • Sixty hours team training to include both *total* in service and combined tactical
    • One hundred hours training each quarter

DEAL WITH THE MEDIA

Hostage and crisis situations seem to attract representatives of the media. Because this is so, we must be prepared to interact effectively with them. Both the police and the media have specific jobs to perform. In some instances, the performance of these jobs creates conflict. Even so, we must learn to work with and around them to accomplish our goals while at the same time finding ways to allow them to do their job. Usually, a department will be well served in this area by appointing a public information officer (PIO) who is directly responsible to the chief or sheriff. Ideally, negotiators should not be involved in media relations or burdened with any of the attendant responsibilities. However, in the real world, hostage negotiators may need to deal with and respond directly to the media. This may include print media, radio, and television. Because this possibility exits, the following guidelines are suggested:

1. If possible, suggest that your department appoint a public information officer who is separate from the negotiations team.
2. Refer all media requests during an incident to the PIO.
3. Avoid providing information directly to the media.
4. Designate a place for all media representatives to assemble.
5. Dispense all information about the incident from the designated media area.
6. Provide light refreshments and bathroom facilities in the designated area.
7. Set regular intervals to provide information. Stay with this schedule.
8. When giving information to the press, only relate current developments to avoid having to remember what was said earlier.
9. Plan for the media with preprepared media releases.
10. Prepare for media encounter by using the "five by five" plan. Plan the answers for the five questions that you hope the media will ask, and for the five questions that you hope the media will not ask.
11. Do not allow the media in the tactical or negotiations command post.

12. Post guards on the commands posts if needed to prevent intrusions.
13. When speaking to the media, tell them what you would like them to know rather than responding to "sound bite" questions. Preplanning will help you to do this effectively.
14. Do not say, "no comment."
15. If you do not know the answer, say that you do not know.
16. If you cannot answer a question, say that you cannot answer the question.
17. Avoid being antagonistic.
18. Move the media to more advantageous positions for pictures, tape, and live coverage as is possible, and only if all safety concerns are met. Tell them that you will do this and then keep your promise.
19. Be careful of "off-the-record" comments made to the media.
20. Do not allow the media access to areas that would not be accessible to the general public under these conditions.
21. Report problems encountered with members of the media to the public information officer or chief of police.
22. Do not make promises of exclusivity.
23. Treat all fairly and consistently.
24. Be sure that you are in control of the incident rather than relinquishing control to the media. It can easily happen.
25. Do not allow the media to tape or to record live, ongoing negotiations.
26. As possible, help the media to do their job. Insist that they not hinder you in doing yours.
27. Avoid allowing the media to inject themselves as intermediaries in the situation.
28. Do not release any information to the media that you would not like the hostage taker or barricaded subject to know.
29. If power remains on in a stronghold, consider that the subject may have access to media reports.
30. If the telephone lines have not been captured by the police, consider that the subject may have direct access to the media.
31. Enlist the help of the media as needed to acquire important information that may help negotiations.
32. Ask the media to inform the public of any specific dangers or safety concerns.

33. Inform the media about the confines of the ongoing situation. Let them know those points beyond which they must not go.
34. Provide regular media updates.
35. Enlist the media's cooperation in not releasing any information that could prove detrimental to the successful outcome of the incident.
36. Ask the media not to broadcast live shots of SWAT positions or of specific police responses.
37. Arrange for interview access to the incident commander as possible.
38. After the incident has been resolved, consider arranging supervised media access to the incident location. Violation of the crime scene must be avoided.
39. Provide a postincident news release. Coordinate this with the incident commander.
40. If negotiators are asked to be interviewed, the interview should be voluntary and include the entire team. Negotiations is a team effort; not an individual event.
41. As possible, be conscious of media deadlines. They have a job to do too.
42. Never avoid the media.
43. Do not discriminate against members of the media.
44. Always be informed.
45. Do not fabricate details to the media.
46. Do not exaggerate.
47. Do not say publicly anything that you do not want on the record.
48. In your statements, do not ramble.
49. Provide solid, concrete information.
50. Avoid trying to take on the media.
51. Do not use the media to engage in public debate.
52. Do not be inconsiderate of the media's need for access to those who have the facts that the media needs.
53. Avoid preconceived bias about the media.
54. Remember that anything that you say to the media represents the entire law enforcement community as well as hostage negotiators.
55. Always present yourself in a professional manner.

56. Verify with the incident commander all information to be released.
57. In anticipation of media questions, gather facts carefully. The "who, what, where, when, why, and how" method usually works well.
58. Arrange a comfortable place for a media briefing.
59. Assist the media in arranging sleeping arrangements if involved in a prolonged operation.
60. Talk to the reporter, not to the microphone or to the camera.
61. Use plain English. Avoid police jargon.
62. Speak slowly and with authority.
63. Use normal voice inflections. Avoid speaking in a monotone.
64. Most in the media want to report correct information. Help them when you can.

Chapter 2

First-Response Duties

The following is provided as a guide to developing standing operating procedures for officers responding to hostage, barricaded, suicidal, and domestic situations. These procedures should be utilized prior to the advent of negotiators and SWAT officers. What is done for the first forty-five minutes to an hour or so, can be the difference between success and failure. If many mistakes are made up front, negotiators must correct those errors before they can move forward to resolve the situation. Much less is made of the role of the first response officer than should be made. This officer(s) may well be key to the overall outcome. This must be emphasized in training and in actual operations. Few are as important to both negotiators and to SWAT.

FOLLOW THE STEPS FOR FIRST RESPONSE

Thirty Steps for Successfully Responding to a Hostage, Barricaded, Suicidal, or Domestic Situation

1. Take charge of the scene until relieved. You have both authority and responsibility for that scene. And it is yours until you are duly relieved. What happens is up to you.
2. Set in motion the department's response mechanism. This is done, in part, by requesting that the SWAT/tactical section and crisis/hostage negotiators be notified and are enroute with the resources relative to the particular situation.
3. Keep the situation from escalating. Avoid anything that would raise the stress level either inside or out. Reassure and calm all concerned. Do not do anything precipitous. Listen to what the subject may say to you and record that information, if possible.

4. Establish an initial inner perimeter that will allow safe maximum observation of the stronghold including coverage of the most likely route of escape. Your patrol procedures will serve you well here. Stay out of harm's way and keep others safe also.

5. Provide necessary information to responding patrol units and tactical elements including the safest route of approach to the scene and to the initial command post. You are in the best position to know what you want and how you want it deployed. Take charge until you are relieved. If you do not, it will not happen.

6. Give guidance, if time permits, for the development of the outer perimeter. You may not have time for this, but keep it in mind if you are asked or if the need arises.

7. Ensure officer safety at all times for all involved personnel. Heroics are out of place here. Safety for all concerned is paramount.

8. If possible, avoid contact with the subject(s). This is especially true in actual hostage situations. Even then, you may not be able to avoid all contact. Avoiding contact is probably not as helpful in suicidal and domestic situations.

9. Use unavoidable contact with the subject to calm and to distract, and to gain both information and time. If contact is made, do a lot of listening to what is said. Reassure the suspect that if he or she keeps things calm and safe on the inside, that you will do the same on the outside.

10. Avoid soliciting demands. Do not ask the subject what he or she wants or what you can get for him or her. Let the subject come to you. If the subject does make demands, take them seriously, write them down, and tell the subject that you will pass his or her wishes along and see what can be done about them.

11. Listen carefully for clues regarding the emotional state of the subject. What he or she says or does can help a lot in determining his or her mental state. Note what is said or observed.

12. Avoid bargaining or making concessions. This is the job of the negotiators. Do not get involved in this area.

13. Reassure the subject that the police will not assault the stronghold. You can do this knowing that if the subject works with us, we will do everything that we can to work with the subject.

14. Avoid offering anything to the subject. Listen to what he or she asks of us. If the subject wants something, he or she will ask.
15. Avoid giving orders to the subject. Do not do this even though you may be tempted. The results could be very bad, especially during the early hours of the situation.
16. Minimize the seriousness of the subject's crimes. Everybody thinks that he or she knows the law. Your knowledge in this area can be conveyed authoritatively and can let the subject know how to help himself or herself.
17. Continue to gather intelligence information concerning such things as the registrations of cars in the area, civilians present, witnesses to the incident, layout of the stronghold, weapons displayed or used, violence threatened or displayed, clothing descriptions for subjects and hostages, movement observed, and any other pertinent information. Even partial information will be helpful to SWAT and to negotiators.
18. Report to the permanent command post for debriefing when relieved. If this is not possible, notify the command post of your location for later debriefing. Do not underestimate the value of the information that you have. We need it. If this is your beat, or an area that you happen to know well, what you have to tell negotiators and SWAT is invaluable.
19. Avoid referring to the persons being held as "hostages." Some people respond negatively to loaded words. Avoid them as much as possible.
20. Avoid attempting to trick the subject. Negotiations and negotiators are not about tricking anyone. Trust and rapport are the real keys. Do not do anything that might cause trust problems later.
21. Strive for honesty with the taker. The general rule is to try to avoid telling lies to the subject. If you must lie, be sure that you cannot get caught doing it by the subject. If you do, your credibility and perhaps that of the negotiators may be lost. In addition, if you must lie, lie only about large things and never about small things. It is one thing to tell the subject that you are working on getting the ten million dollars. It is quite another to promise to deliver a sandwich and then fail to deliver it.

22. Refrain from encouraging hostages to escape. People may get hurt unnecessarily this way. Better for them to stay put and let us get them all out in a safe manner. Some will escape anyway. All the better. Just do not encourage it. In the alternative, encourage them to stay where they are and to know that help is on the way.

23. Avoid giving a "no" response to a demand. "No" conveys a certain finality that may lead to other unfortunate actions because of the subject's mental state. Better to say "I'll check" or "I will find out" than to give an outright no.

24. Avoid making suggestions. This is not the time for that and you may come across as sounding parental or accusatory. Police officers have this tendency anyway. Hold off here.

25. Avoid allowing outsiders, nonpolice, family members, psychologists, psychiatrists, clergy, and any other nontrained, nonpolice negotiators from talking to the subject. All professionals have their professional agenda. These may be inappropriate in this type of police situation and could make matters a lot worse. Family members may be part of the problem.

26. Never exchange yourself or anyone else for a hostage. Although this sounds like a good idea to many police officers, do not do it. The horror stories go on and on about situations in which these types of exchanges were made. It is not a good idea here.

27. Ask if the subject intends to kill himself or herself if you suspect that he or she is suicidal. Asking a person if he or she is suicidal will not put the idea of suicide in his or her head. If the person is suicidal, the idea is already there. If not, he or she will tell you and you can evaluate from there. If a person is suicidal, your willingness to be open and honest about the subject may not only allow him or her to speak openly about his or her plans, but may also help in establishing rapport between the two of you. This rapport may help resolve the situation favorably.

28. Protect yourself from becoming vulnerable to injury by never talking with a subject while you are unprotected and exposed to danger. In the vernacular of the negotiator, "face to face" does not really mean facing off with the subject. It has a particular meaning that ensures the safety of all concerned. If you

are unexpectedly caught in such a situation, do the best you can.

29. Be aware of the changing circumstances within the scene and make the necessary notifications. Try to let those involved know what is going on.

30. Coordinate with fire and emergency medical personnel at the scene. Keep them advised of the situation as appropriate and as time permits. If you can do this, it will help. If fact, such coordination may be handled by supervisors and the tactical unit as the situation progresses.

DEVELOP INTELLIGENCE AT THE SCENE

Initial intelligence sets the stage for what will come after. The following information, to be gathered by the first responding officers, is essential to the overall effort of resolving these types of situations. Gather as much as you can and as you have the time to do it. Even partial information is helpful. Get whatever you can get and report it, including all of the following:

Date of incident
Service or offense number
Name of subject
Race of subject
Sex of subject
Height
Weight
Color of eyes
Color of hair
Current clothing
Demands made
Type of incident
Address of incident
Phone number of stronghold
Weapons suspected or displayed
Suspect vehicles
Possible motive
History of medical problems

History of substance abuse
Military history
Marital information and history
Religious background
Criminal history
Personality traits
Suicidal behavior
Behavior of subject at this scene
Behavior of this subject at previous scenes
Layout/map of the stronghold with structural details
Similar information on any hostages or detained persons involved
Clothing description for each hostage
Relationship to hostage taker or person detaining of each person
detained
Mental status and personality traits of the hostages
Location and status of any noncombatants trapped within the
perimeters
Name, badge number, and unit of first-responding officer gathering this information

GATHER IMPORTANT INFORMATION IMMEDIATELY IN HOSTAGE AND BARRICADE SITUATIONS

For the first responders, certain initial information becomes important to ascertain immediately. Negotiators and SWAT may need this
information upon arrival at the scene.

- Identity of subject
- Description of subject
- Possible motive
- Hostage information
    —Hostage number one
    —Hostage number two
    —Hostage number three
- Weapons information
- Level of violence displayed or threatened
- Structural details of stronghold

- Position of all officers
- Location of noncombatants within the inner perimeter
- Map/sketch of stronghold
- Map/sketch of incident area

Chapter 3

Callout Response

Callouts can come at the most inconvenient times. They come when you are tired, sleeping, eating a meal with your family, or attending your child's school performance, and probably the last thing you want to do is go to work for another several hours. But be ready. This is what often happens. If you are going to be a negotiator, expect that the callouts will come inconveniently and that you will be expected to perform at 100 percent efficiency at the scene. No one cares that you are tired and have other things to do or that you have not had a callout in a long time and your skills are a bit rusty. All anyone cares about is that you do your job with the same skill and talent that would be expected of someone who did nothing else every day but negotiate for people's lives. It is what you signed on for, and you are going to do the job this time just as you have in the past. The goal always is the same: Preserve life by negotiating for as long as that life is worth. The following are a few guidelines that may help you prepare and respond.

KEEP EQUIPMENT PREPARED

1. Keep your negotiator's equipment within arm's reach at all times.
2. Keep equipment and gear in your primary callout vehicle so that you will not have to worry that you have everything you need when under the pressure of being summoned.
3. Reorganize your personal equipment on a regular basis. Allow for seasonal changes.
4. Take your negotiator's equipment seriously just as any specialized team would. I will bet you that SWAT takes their equipment very seriously.
5. Keep an up-to-date map or directions finder with your equipment.

PREPARE YOUR FAMILY

Explain to your significant others the special responsibilities of your job.

PREPARE YOURSELF

1. Expect to be called at unusual and inconvenient times.
2. When called after you have been asleep, be sure that you are awake before receiving the information from the caller. After the call, do not go back to sleep.
3. Even though you will try to respond to the callout quickly, take care of personal needs before leaving the house. These might include routine medications, personal hygiene, attention to bodily functions, etc. They may be harder to take care of on scene.
4. Be sure to bring medications, both prescription and non-prescription, that you may need if the incident is lengthy.
5. Maintain your own physical fitness. You need this just as much as the SWAT team does.
6. Keep your pager and/or cell phone with you at all times. Your troubles are just beginning if you cannot be reached.
7. Take alternate clothing to account for changes in venue and in weather. On a cold night, for example, do not assume that you will be negotiating from inside a warm building. Situations change, and so must you.
8. Take fresh, healthy food and drinks with you, if you have time, to supplement that which you should carry routinely in your equipment.
9. If you have responsibilities for bringing team equipment to the scene, do not forget. The absence of necessary personal and team equipment will create problems and delays.
10. Refer to the lists within this book to see what personal equipment you should assemble.
11. Provide for your personal needs while on scene. A large plastic jar will be quite helpful, for example, if you have to urinate and restrooms are not available.
12. Have with you whatever you need to function in any position on the negotiations team when you arrive on scene.

RESPOND TO THE SCENE

1. When called, be sure that you get all of the information that you need in order to respond to the scene appropriately.
2. Write down information transmitted to you by dispatch or by the team leader.
3. If enough information is not given, ask for it.
4. Dress for the particular conditions under which you will be operating in a given situation.
5. Find out where to report and the best way to get there.
6. Respond to the scene as quickly and as safely as possible. If you do not get there, you cannot help.
7. Monitor the appropriate radio frequencies and respond as called.
8. Because dedicated frequencies are usually busy during an incident, stay off the air as much as possible.
9. Respond to the scene in the authorized team or departmental uniform or distinctive clothing.
10. Before responding to the scene, and after arriving on the scene, evaluate the situation so that you can be adequately prepared for what follows.
11. If, during your response to the scene, you encounter the media, refer them to the public information officer of your department or other designated official. Do not give your own statement without authorization.
12. At the scene, park your vehicle appropriately close to the command post or where designated for easy equipment access and safety.

REPORT TO THE COMMAND POST

1. Know where the negotiations command post is located.
2. Know where the tactical command post is located.
3. When you arrive on the scene, report to the team leader or senior team member.
4. Determine your job for this incident.
5. Do not delay in beginning your assignment. Report your progress to the team leader.

6. Refer to your training notes and to your negotiator's notebook to be sure that you are accomplishing all needed aspects of your job assignment.
7. Leave nothing to chance.
8. Avoid the junk food that is usually present at an incident.
9. Plan to be involved in the incident for many hours. Assume such a situation could go for a very long time. If not, so much the better. Don't anticipate an early resolution.
10. Be a team player at all times.
11. Recognize that tempers may flare as time goes on and others get tired.
12. Help with decision making.
13. Strive to "keep your head about you."
14. Rest when you can.
15. Pay close attention to instructions given to you by the team leader.
16. Assist in setting up equipment such as hostage phones, monitors, radios, etc.
17. Assume command of, and responsibility for, the team if you are the senior team member.
18. Be aware of sources of relevant intelligence.
19. Be prepared to make contact with the hostage taker or crisis victim without delay if appropriate and indicated.
20. Enjoy your role as a negotiator. Learn from it. Remember that your job is one of the most important and highly skilled in your department. You might be surprised to know that many do not know that fact. Negotiators may feel underappreciated by their department and by those they serve. Negotiators do what they do because they know that it is often essential to life.

Chapter 4

Arriving on Scene and Setting Up

ORGANIZE PERSONNEL AT THE SCENE

Organization at the scene, and especially negotiations team organization, must be carefully planned and understood. In addition, the juxtaposition of the negotiations team to the other active components must be considered to ensure success for all involved. (Refer to the command post structure example in Figure 4.1. Specific command post structure will be determined by the needs, capabilities, and resources of individual units. Also, the major components and responsibilities of a negotiations team are detailed in Chapter 5.) There are many ways to organize a hostage and crisis negotiations team. Whatever way is chosen should reflect the needs and style of your team, the number of team members, and the guidelines of your organization. If it reflects how you operate, it will be more successful than if you base your organization on how other teams do it.

REMAIN AWARE OF LEGAL CONSIDERATIONS

The importance of understanding the legalities attached to crisis negotiations should not be underestimated. In our world, even the best plans and procedures can and will come under close scrutiny. Although experience shows that concern about these areas is not the central focus for most police negotiators, knowing how the law applies to this particular arena can do nothing but strengthen a negotiator's professionalism. The law is important from at least two perspectives: (1) knowledge of the law that will help with the actual negotiations with a subject, and (2) understanding of the laws that may affect how we establish negotiations and what we can and cannot do.

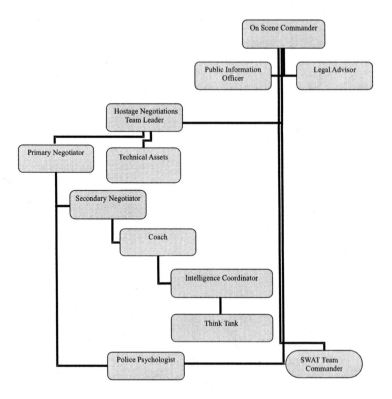

FIGURE 4.1. Command Post Structure Example

Legal Guidelines for Crisis Intervention

1. Always treat people as human beings, not just as cases.
2. Show respect to all with whom you are involved.
3. Intervene within the limits of your background and training. Do not exceed those limits. Ask for help when needed. Recognize your own limitations.
4. Unless you must intervene (e.g., no one else is available), consider carefully whether you want to perform an intervention. Discuss this with your team leader.
5. Once you have begun to intervene, don't stop unless directed to do so by the team leader.

6. Discontinue your intervention only if you are relieved by someone with greater skill or resources than your own.
7. Determine how, and if, the Good Samaritan Laws relate to the types of intervention in which you may be involved.
8. If in doubt about your legal standing, contact a competent attorney and discuss your concerns. The departmental legal advisor can be a good resource if he or she is familiar with hostage, barricaded, and crisis situations within the police venue.
9. Maintain confidentiality of all information you obtain about a crisis victim. Understand under what special circumstances you may have a duty to warn another person or to otherwise breach intervener-victim confidentiality.
10. Document everything you say and do with a victim. This may assist you later if you or your procedures are challenged. Taping negotiations or interventions may help in this regard.
11. Maintain your competency. Update your training and credentials as required.
12. Whenever possible, obtain the victim's consent before you assist with the crisis. If in doubt, ask! Taking time to do this will enhance your credibility with the subject.
13. If emergency circumstances do not allow for actual consent by the victim, you may be able to proceed under the concept of implied consent. However, in such circumstances, do only what is absolutely necessary to effectively intervene.
14. Do not disturb a crime scene. If you cannot avoid doing so, note the exact location of whatever is moved so that later you can give such information to investigators.
15. If you must search a victim's personal effects, try to have one or two witnesses present to observe your actions. Know the laws and policies that govern what you can and cannot do.
16. Know what you are required to report.
17. Know the legal procedures in your jurisdiction for admissions for psychiatric care. Usually admissions are categorized as either voluntary or involuntary.
18. Remember that crisis interveners and negotiators are not usually immune from observation of motor vehicle laws or from legal responsibility for vehicular accidents or property damage. Know the laws and your department's policy.

19. Respect the victim's right to privacy.
20. If the victim is a minor, obtain the permission of one of the parents before intervening. If this is not possible, you may be able to proceed under the doctrine of implied consent, as you would with an adult.
21. Be honest and open with victims.
22. Always think through what you will do, toward what end you will be doing it, what risks are present, and what safeguards you will apply.
23. Prepare yourself with knowledge of the law as well as of crisis intervention skills.
24. Remember that liability can be affected by both acts of commission and acts of omission.
25. Respect a sufferer's right to refuse your intervention. In a barricade situation, acknowledge his or her right to refuse help, but keep trying.
26. Before entering a crisis victim's domain, dwelling, or office, request that person's permission. Know when the laws of your locality permit you to enter without permission.
27. If you are the supervisor of crisis interveners or negotiators, be sure all interveners understand and can apply agency policies and procedures.
28. Within agency and team, develop specific, understandable policies and procedures that clearly regulate and illustrate how intervention is to be performed.
29. As a supervisor, adhere to agency policy and insist that interveners/negotiators do likewise.
30. Incorporate agency policies and legal issues into the training of crisis interveners and negotiators.

Case Law

The following are several of the laws that may have relevance to hostage and crisis negotiations specifically. Most have relevance to other areas of police work also. However, the information provided is drafted for use by negotiators.

Fourth Amendment (Search and Seizure): Emergency Searches

Mincy v. Arizona, 437U.S.385(1978)—Warrantless entry into a house to aid an officer involved in a gunfight was lawful. However, a subsequent three-day search for evidence was unlawful because it was conducted without a warrant.

Vale v. Louisiana, 399U.S.30(1970); Schmerber v. California, 384U.S.757(1966)—Warrantless searches to prevent the imminent destruction of evidence is lawful if the scope of the search is confined to the exigencies necessitating the search.

Warden v. Hayden, 387U.S.294(1967)—Warrantless entry to arrest following the hot pursuit of a suspect is lawful. In addition, until the suspect is located, a search of the house may be conducted for the suspect and dangerous weapons the suspect is known to possess.

Statements Made During the Negotiations

Statements made during the negotiations process are arguably not governed by *Miranda* because they are made in noncustodial settings or not in response to interrogation.

New York v. Quarles, 104S.Ct.2626(1984)—Questions reasonably prompted by concerns for public safety are not governed by the *Miranda* rules, and any statements made in response are admissible in evidence.

United States v. Mesa, 638F.2d582(3rd Cir.1980)—Telephone negotiations for release of hostages with a man barricaded inside his or her home do not require the admonition of *Miranda* rights. Since the FBI was not in control of the setting, timing, or content of the discussions, and did not have immediate control over the subject, *Miranda* does not apply. An opposite rule would not be logical: When confronted with an armed barricaded suspect who is possibly holding hostages, the negotiator's attention would be diverted from what should be his or her primary purpose of using the means most likely to convince the subject to surrender peacefully without harming anyone else in the area. The negotiator would be forced to consider the possibility that the suspect might make a statement that the government eventually would want to introduce at trial. Then, he or she would have to assess whether the subject would be likely to react violently to the antagonistic-sounding *Miranda* warnings.

State v. Sands, 700P.2d1369(Ariz.App.1985)—We cannot find that a man in his own home, possessing weapons, food, and supplies, with a vehicle at his disposal, a telephone and resisting arrest can be said to be in custody.

People v. Gantz, 480N.Y.S.2d583(N.Y.Sup.Ct.1984)—Even assuming that the defendant was in custody during the hostage negotiations . . . the negotiations were directed toward providing the defendant with medication and maintaining the hostage's safety, not to elicit inculpatory statements. . . . Despite the lack of *Miranda* warnings, the trial court did not err in refusing to suppress those statements.

Promises of Leniency

United States v. Crosby, 713F.2d1066(5th Cir.1983)—The jury is not entitled to hear a portion of tape recording of hostage negotiations that promised the defendant that he would not be prosecuted if he released hostages. This is because it might induce unnecessary sympathy. However, if the defendant could establish its relevance, the entire tape could be played.

State v. Sands, 700P2d1369(Ariz.App.1985)—A purported letter of immunity signed by the sheriff was void since it was given under duress. A contract induced by duress is unenforceable.

Electronic Surveillance

Title III, 18U.S.C.2510 et seq. determined the following:

- Consensual monitoring is not covered by this statute.
- Nonconsensual monitoring of telephone conversations requires either a court order, routine monitoring by law en-

forcement authorities, or an emergency threatening immediate danger of death or serious physical injury.

- Nonconsensual monitoring by mechanical device of oral conversations requires either a court order, the absence of a reasonable expectation of privacy, or an emergency threatening immediate danger of death or serious physical injury.
- All emergency electronic surveillance must be followed by the application and order within forty-eight hours whether or not interceptions occurred.

Katz v. United States, 389U.S.347(1967)

Cusumano v. United States, 67F.3d1497(10thCir.1995); Affirmed on rehearing, 83F3d1247(10thCir.1996)

Porco v. United States, 842F.Supp.1393(D.Wyo.1994)

Kyllo v. United States, WLS.C.998508 Argued February 20, 2001. Decided June 11, 2001

Government Liability

The Federal Tort Claims Act (FTCA) is the U.S. government's waiver of sovereign immunity for certain acts of its employees. The U.S. government can be held liable for the negligence of its employees.

U.S. v. Downs, 522F.2d990(6th Cir.1975)—The United States is liable under the FTCA when FBI ASAC failed to follow the FBI's policy for the resolution of an airplane hijacking. The FBI agent is required to exercise the highest degree of care commensurate with all facts within his or her knowledge.

31 U.S.C.3274—The U.S. government may pay claims up to $50,000 for its nonnegligent acts.

Individual Liability

Daniels v. Williams, 106S.Ct.662(1986)—Negligence is not actionable under section 1983 (Bivens litigation).

Whitley v. Albers, 106S.Ct.1078(1986)—Prison officials who use force to quell a disturbance are not liable unless they acted maliciously and sadistically for the very purpose of causing harm. Only unnecessary and wanton infliction of pain upon prisoners is unlawful.

Hudson v. McMillian, 112S.Ct.995(1992)—Under the Cruel and Unusual Punishment Clause, the key inquiry is whether the force was applied in a good faith effort to maintain and to restore discipline, or maliciously and sadistically to cause harm. The amount of force and the seriousness of the injury in relationship to the threat perceived by prison officials are relevant factors. However, where there is no justified need, and officials maliciously and sadistically use force to cause harm, the Eighth Amendment is violated whether or not significant injury resulted. This is so unless the injury was truly de minimis and was not the sort that is repugnant to the conscience of mankind.

Taylor v. Watters, 655F.Supp.801(E.D. Mich.1987)—It is the nature of police work that the pressure becomes intense and decisions must be made quickly. Decisions of police officers on the scene may be questioned after the fact, but the decision made on the spot does not permit such reflections. Inevitably, police officers make mistakes. Such mistakes made in the best judgment of the trained police officer should not be the province of constitutional tort suits.

Salas v. Carpenter, 980F.2d299(5th Cir.1992)—Sheriff who refused to allow the use of a city SWAT team and hostage negotiators, but instead used his deputies who were not SWAT trained, or trained in hostage negotiations, was not liable when the abductor killed the hostage. The Constitution protects against an abuse of authority, but does not protect persons against private violence. Had the sheriff prevented the hostage's rescue, liability may have attached. However, here the sheriff offered alternative rescue methods, and although not as good, they cannot be said to be grossly negligent or wanton conduct.

Use of Force

Tennessee v. Garner, 105S.Ct.1694(1985)—Deadly force may be used if reasonably necessary for self-protection or the protections of others or to prevent the escape of a dangerous fleeing felon.

Graham v. Connor, 109S.Ct.1865(1989)—The use of non-deadly force is judged by the reasonableness standard of the Fourth Amendment. Three factors are of primary importance: (1)the seriousness of the offense; (2) the threat to the officers; and (3) the degree of resistance offered by the suspect.

Landol-Rivera v. Cruz Cosme, 906F2d791(1st Cir.1990)—The accidental shooting of a hostage as a car was being commandeered by the hostage taker did not constitute a seizure of that person under the Fourth Amendment. Unless the restraint of liberty . . . resulted from an attempt to gain control of the individual . . . there has been no Fourth Amendment seizure. . . . No Fourth Amendment seizure occurred here because Landol was not the object of the police bullet that struck him.

Control of the Media

KOED v. Houchins, 438U.S.1(1978)—The media has no constitutional right to be in areas not accessible to the general public.

Privacy Protection Act, 42U.S.C.2000aa—The government may not seize media work product except under specific circumstances.

Minneapolis Star Tribune *v. United States, Civ. Action No. 3-87-36(D.Minn.1988)*—Agents who seized cameras and film from the media at the scene of an arrest violated the Privacy Protection Act.

Unit Organization

Downs v. United States, 522F.2d990(1975)—Special circumstances require special procedures. Ad hoc approaches are illegal.

City of Winter Haven v. Allen, 541So.2d128(Fla.App.1989) — Reiterated *Downs v. U.S.* Ad hoc approaches to critical incidents are inappropriate.

Personnel Selection

Moon v. Winfield, 383F.Supp.31(1974)—This is not a hostage negotiations case. In personnel selection, characteristics of what is desired in those chosen must be identified. A chief of police was held responsible for choosing a person totally unqualified for the job for which the person was chosen.

Training

City of Canton v. Harris, 489U.S.378,109S.Ct.1197(1989)— Selection should be on basis of ability. Training should be on those tasks that must be performed. Continuous training should be provided.

OBSERVE TELEPHONE SURVEILLANCE GUIDELINES AND LAWS

After reviewing the previous legal guidelines, take time to review the excerpts from the Texas Penal Code and Texas Code of Criminal Procedure specifically concerning the use of communication equipment during a hostage or barricaded situation. Be sure and check your own jurisdiction for local rules. These are located in Appendix IV. Also in Appendix IV is an example of an Order to Consent to Interception of Wire and Oral Communication Sample Pleadings. Again, your local jurisdiction will rule. Please do not disregard these issues. Unfortunately, negotiators do not always take these particular issues seriously. Fortunately, most of the time, the issues are not raised. Unfortunately, if they are ever raised, and you are not prepared, the consequences can be disastrous. Do not let that happen to you, your team, and your department.

SET UP TELEPHONE OR OTHER
COMMUNICATION SYSTEM

Most of the time, you will probably need to establish communication via a telephone system of some type. Occasionally, contact will be made without such aids (e.g., use of a bullhorn or radio). Whatever the system, it should provide for involvement of the entire negotiations team. This is especially true for the primary and secondary negotiator. To establish communication absent the ability of the team to work together limits overall team effectiveness.

The following guidelines may help:

1. Be sure that every member of the negotiations team, regardless of primary function, knows how to assemble all communication equipment.
2. Use team training time to review assembly of communication gear. Such procedures are easy to forget and must not be subject to guesswork when the team is deployed.
3. Avoid the use of devices that do not allow for secure communication, if at all possible.
4. Radio and loudspeaker communication with the hostage taker or victim should be avoided, if possible. If not possible to avoid, they should be used only with careful consideration of the possible consequences.
5. Cell phone contact, although simple to establish, may not allow for team members to work together during the incident. In some instances, cell phones can be monitored by outsiders.
6. Explore commercial hostage and crisis communication systems. Be sure that the one chosen fits your team's needs, capabilities, and financial resources.
7. If you must develop your own system, consult with departmental technicians or other experts for needed assistance.
8. Develop multiple approaches to establishing communication at the scene.
9. Develop procedures for establishing effective communication if you are deployed to more than one incident occurring at the same time.
10. Be sure that communication procedures do not violate Fourth Amendment or other constitutional considerations, state laws, local rules, or departmental policy. See Appendix IV for reference material in these areas.

Chapter 5

Preparing to Negotiate

REVIEW INFORMATION ON THE ABNORMAL PSYCHOLOGY OF HOSTAGE TAKERS

Since the development of modern police hostage negotiations techniques in the 1970s, several typologies have been offered for categorizing hostage takers (Arieti, 1963; Fowler and Greenstone, 1996; Greenstone, 1989, 1998a, 1999; Lanceley, 1981; McMains and Mullins, 1996; Strentz, 1983). For example, some frameworks are based on whether the perpetrator has a mental disorder or is a criminal (in some cases, including an additional category for terrorists); still others emphasize whether the victim is a stranger versus a family member. Negotiations strategies based on these categorizations are utilized by hostage negotiators in guiding their interventions. In recent years, conceptualizations of the hostage taker have been modified and restructured. The newer conceptualizations also include subjects in domestic crises (Fowler, 1997; Fowler and Greenstone, 1989; Greenstone, 1993a; Greenstone and Leviton, 1993, 1996; McMains and Lanceley, 1995). In all cases, an initial assessment and subsequent diagnostic profile is essential for defining the resolution strategies.

One accepted typology for discriminating among hostage takers involves two major categories and at least four subcategories (Bolz, 1979; Cooper, 1997; Fuselier, 1981; Greenstone, 1998a, 1999; Hare, 1995; FBI Instructional Material, FBI Academy, 1984, 1994; Strentz, 1979). As shown in Table 5.1, psychotic disorders are distinguished from personality or character disorders. Psychotic disorders are further divided into paranoid schizophrenia and bipolar disorder. Despite its absence from the DSM-IV (American Psychiatric Association, 1994), the term *manic depression* has been retained as a useful working diagnosis for hostage negotiators (Greenstone, 1998a, 1999;

TABLE 5.1. Classifications of Hostage Takers and Crisis Victims

Classification	Characteristics Taught to Police Negotiators	Negotiations Guidelines
Schizophrenia, paranoid type	Delusions Hallucinations Chemical imbalance Not multiple personality Unrealistic concerns about autonomy Unrealistic concerns about sexual identity Feels controlled by external forces Disturbance of affect Ambivalence Autistic thinking Association difficulties	Do not crowd or stare at the subject Do not offer unrequested intimacy Do not argue with his or her delusions Do not argue with his or her hallucinations Do not attempt mental health intervention Do not insert family members Consider use of opposite-sex negotiators Let him or her talk and establish rapport Ally yourself with the individual Negotiators may be rejected with time Large body space requirement Expect weird demands from this subject
Manic depression—depressed state (bipolar disorder)	Extreme depression Unrealistic sadness and hopelessness Slowed thinking and response Difficulty with thought processes Possibly acutely suicidal	Avoid projecting life into the future Deal in the here and now Beware of sudden improvements in mood May need to wait longer for responses Relatives may escalate feelings of guilt Go slow; develop rapport With rapport, may be more directive Offer reassurance as often as needed Expect honesty from this subject Small body space requirement Demands: "Leave me alone" or "Go away"

Disorder	Characteristics	Strategies
Inadequate personality (DSM-II)	History of problems, often petty in nature History of repeated failures in life Ineffectual responses to life's demands Inadaptability in most areas of life Ineptness and poor judgment Social instability Very manipulative Unable to keep a job and poor planning Sexual irregularities Suicide potential Overuse of fantasy Uses others to get what he or she wants Presents as calm, cool, quiet, and polite Strong bonding under traumatic situations	Do not use nonpolice negotiators Show understanding Build self-esteem Provide uncritical acceptance Consider opposite-sex negotiators With rapport, may be more directive Subject may not want incident to end May have a problem with loyalty Demands may be exorbitant

TABLE 5.1 *(continued)*

Classification	Characteristics Taught to Police Negotiators	Negotiations Guidelines
Antisocial personality	Asocial	Do not get into a contest of wills
	Amoral	Do not use nonpolice negotiators
	Short-run hedonist	Nonpolice may worsen situation
	Inability to sustain work relationships	Do not expect interpersonal bonding
	Knows the rules; they do not apply to him or her	Ego stimulation and ego threat motivate
	Lacks ability to be responsible parent	Remember subject's egocentricity
	Fails to accept social norms	Release of hostages to subject's gain
	Unable to keep lasting personal relations	Keep subject in problem-solving mode
	Self-centered	Negotiations should be reality oriented
	Out for self to point of hurting others	Tactical intervention may be needed
	Makes a model prisoner	Demands will be realistic and precise
	Very manipulative	
	May end up interviewing the negotiator	
	High verbal skills	
	Blames others for his or her problems	
	May be very cool and calculating	

FBI Instructional Material, FBI Academy, 1984, 1994). Generally, hostage negotiators have been confronted with the manic-depressive individual in the depressed state (Greenstone, 1998a).

Character disorders are subdivided into the *inadequate personality* and the *antisocial personality*. Even though inadequate personality is not an accepted DSM-IV diagnosis (APA, 1994), it has demonstrated usefulness in discriminating among hostage takers.

REVIEW NEGOTIATIONS STRATEGIES

As portrayed in Table 5.1, field diagnoses inform negotiations strategies. For example, the approach effective with the highly depressed and suicidal individual may prove much less useful with the psychotic or antisocial subject. Although there are still some who take the "shotgun" approach to negotiations, the more refined the diagnosis and understanding of the subject involved, the more accurate and precise can be the negotiations strategies. For instance, although problems sustaining effective work relationships are common to inadequate and antisocial personalities, knowing that the underlying difficulties are vastly different in these subjects can be very useful. The overwhelming nature of the work environment for the inadequate personality is quite different from a work environment in constant turmoil due to the actions of the antisocial subject. Whereas the former frequently quits the job, the latter often gets fired. Understanding such nuances may help to select strategies in negotiating with these individuals. For example, the former subject may need the reassurance of the negotiator that he or she is doing the best that he or she can despite his or her sense of repeated failures. The latter may need to be approached with ego-enhancing statements that reinforce his or her self-concept. For instance, it might be suggested that it is the employer's fault, not the subject's, that he or she was fired.

Exceptions to the classifications in Table 5.1 are also seen in the field and are considered when training negotiators. Many who suffer from depression are not bipolar, but are reacting to a specific loss in their lives (reactive depression) or experiencing a unipolar major depression. Also, not all persons who commit crimes are antisocial, as previously described. Some petty criminals are prompted by their circumstances to take hostages to use as leverage against the police. For example, a subject surprised in the act of robbery may take a hostage to use as a shield. The primary motive may have been robbery, not hostage taking. In addition, diagnostic characteristics may overlap somewhat in profiling actual subjects, and negotiators should expect this (Biggs, 1987; Davis, 1987; Dolan and Fuselier, 1989; Fuselier, 1986; Soskis and Van Zandt, 1986; Wesselius, 1983).

Hostage Negotiations Field Assessment

It is necessary to understand that police negotiators have many and varied responsibilities, and the development of perpetrator profiles is only one of several simultaneous responsibilities of the hostage negotiations team members. Police negotiators operate as members of specially trained teams with both discrete and overlapping responsibilities (see Table 5.2). The broad scope of their duties and responsibilities requires knowledge and abilities both unique to police and common to other negotiations situations. Moreover, an officer's specific role on the negotiations team may vary from one incident to another, depending on characteristics of the situation, availability of other personnel, and preferences of the team leader.

The organization of a police negotiations team can take various forms. The model depicted in Table 5.2 is widely used to address the

TABLE 5.2. Hostage Negotiations Team Job Assignments

Job Number	Assignment	Duties
1	Primary negotiator	Negotiates with subject
2	Secondary negotiator	Assists #1; listens to negotiations; gathers intelligence
3	Coach/police psychologist	Monitors negotiations; provides input to negotiators
4	Intelligence coordinator	Gathers, evaluates, and disseminates intelligence; provides plans and strategies
5	Negotiations team leader	Runs team; coordinates with SWAT
N/A	Technicians	Maintain, install, and repair negotiations equipment

core responsibilities of the hostage negotiations team. This basic structure can also be modified to meet the needs of specific teams under special conditions, and within the confines of a specific police department. Nevertheless, some negotiations teams will define themselves differently than as presented here and may use other names for the different jobs performed. It may be important to note that the organization of negotiations teams in this country is under study by the FBI, and current discussions suggest that direction is emerging that may affect current structure. This may include revising the structure of the team and also the utilization of personnel. However, regardless of titles or structure, the goals will remain the same: to get everyone out safely.

A negotiations team may comprise as few as one or two members, particularly in small departments that cannot dedicate more to this function. Indeed, in some incidents, a smaller team can be as effective as a larger team. However, where possible, a team of at least five members is advantageous for distributing the different responsibilities. Some teams will utilize more negotiators as a function of the nature of the incident. For example, an incident that lasts an extended period of time may require more personnel. A more complex terrorist incident may require more negotiators for input or for separate negotiations. Nevertheless, the five-person structure provides a useful vehicle for summarizing the chief roles and responsibilities of the hostage negotiations team.

Within the framework of the five-person team, the primary negotiator assumes the major responsibility for interacting with the hostage taker or crisis victim. All other jobs on the team are devoted to supporting the role of this negotiator. The secondary negotiator is responsible for assisting the primary negotiator and for assuring that all intelligence information directed to the primary is conveyed in a timely and efficient manner. This negotiator also monitors all negotiations and substitutes for the primary as needed.

The coach provides a third set of ears in the negotiations room, and this person may be utilized in various additional capacities at the request of the primary negotiator (e.g., maintaining the negotiations log or conveying information to the intelligence coordinator or team leader). This third person may also be the police psychologist in departments providing such services. He or she monitors the stress level of the primary and the hostage taker, usually referred to as the subject, and is available to provide perspective and input.

The intelligence coordinator is the recipient, repository, and developer of intelligence information gathered during an incident. Such information may then be further developed into specific negotiations strategies to be used by the primary negotiator. This is the person who would normally be responsible for gathering the information needed for completing field diagnostic assessments. Because complete information about the subject is not usually available, the intelligence coordinator is responsible for inserting additional information as it becomes available. Logs and records are also maintained at this level.

The person in charge of the overall functions of the negotiations team is the negotiations team leader. He or she must ensure the efficient functioning of the team while at the same time be available to liaise with the other teams and elements of command that are involved. These may include the special weapons and tactics team and the incident command staff. The overall efficiency of the negotiations team depends on how well this job is performed.

As with most crises, hostage crises seldom occur when you are expecting them and are rested and ready. Callouts to sensitive and potentially deadly situations can occur at any time and usually do. Table 5.3 describes the multiple facets of a typical police hostage or crisis situation. It also shows the polyphasic nature of police negotiations. However, it should be kept in mind that the procedures listed here may be modified depending on the specific situation. It should also be underscored that the intelligence function responsible for developing the data for diagnostic assessments is only one of many responsibilities assumed by members of the negotiations team. Successful resolution of any incident requires global knowledge of the sequencing and the skills to perform at any level as the need arises. These requirements for broad knowledge, readiness for action, and flexibility clearly differentiate the hostage negotiations situation from most other negotiations situations.

Table 5.3. Typical Resolution Steps for Police Hostage and Crisis Situations

Sequence	Specific Time-Related Segments
First	The initial callout at anytime, day or night
Second	Response of SWAT and negotiators
Third	Arrival of SWAT and securing scene
Fourth	Arrival and setup of negotiations team
Fifth	Initial gathering of intelligence information
Sixth	Preparations by negotiations team
Seventh	Ongoing intelligence gathering
Eighth	Coordination with SWAT commander
Ninth	Initial contact between negotiator and subject
Tenth	Attempts to establish rapport with subject
Eleventh	Initial profiling of hostage taker or victim
Twelfth	In-depth intelligence gathering
Thirteenth	Evaluation of intelligence material
Fourteenth	Goal setting by negotiations team
Fifteenth	Continuing negotiations based on strategies
Sixteenth	Continued profiling/check of mental status
Seventeenth	Confirmation of initial observations
Eighteenth	Threat assessment
Nineteenth	Assessment of needs and interests
Twentieth	Information sharing with SWAT
Twenty-first	Bargaining or crisis intervention
Twenty-second	Problem solving and rapport building
Twenty-third	Development of surrender plan
Twenty-fourth	Orchestration of surrender with the subject
Twenty-fifth	Execution of surrender plan with SWAT
Twenty-sixth	Subject taken into custody
Twenty-seventh	Decision making regarding disposition
Twenty-eighth	Postincident interviews with subject
Twenty-ninth	Postincident interviews with hostages
Thirtieth	Negotiations team debriefing
Thirty-first	Full tactical debriefing
Thirty-second	Training for future incidents

Chapter 6

Making Contact
and Beginning Negotiations

KNOW THE STAGES OF NEGOTIATIONS

When speaking of hostage negotiations, it is easy to assume that there is an all-encompassing, singular process called "negotiations." Actually, what we casually refer to as hostage and crisis negotiations is really a series of steps. One of those steps in the process is the actual "negotiations" or bargaining. Other stages must have been resolved prior to the advent of actual negotiations in order for this stage to be successful. In addition, there are stages that must be completed postnegotiations in order to ensure ultimate success and crisis resolution.

These stages are not static. They may change as situations change. Additional steps may be required. Fewer steps may be used as appropriate. The following should serve as a guide only.

Stage One: Preplanning
Stage Two: Initial incident
Stage Three: Gathering intelligence
Stage Four: Establishing contact
Stage Five: Building rapport
Stage Six: Negotiations/bargaining
Stage Seven: Problem solving
Stage Eight: Dealing with objections
Stage Nine: The surrender
Stage Ten: Debriefing

REVIEW THE GREENSTONE MODEL OF CRISIS INTERVENTION

1. *Immediacy:* Action must be taken now.
2. *Control:* The negotiator or intervener must provide structure and support for the subject and for the situation.
3. *Assessment:* Often missed even by experienced interveners. You must know what it is that presents in front of you before you can make an effective decision about what to do.
4. *Disposition:* Once you know what you have, then you can do what is needed to resolve or to manage the incident: negotiate or intervene in a crisis.
5. *Referral:* Sometimes help is needed beyond the initial intervention. If you have done the previous steps effectively, the possibility of a successful referral increases.
6. *Follow-up:* This is probably the hardest step to follow. Time and other duties often prevent us from finding out what actually happened to the victim or hostage taker. One great benefit of the follow-up is that it may provide significant information about the effectiveness of the intervention and provide material that can be duplicated in training.

DETERMINE WHETHER YOU HAVE A HOSTAGE OR CRISIS SITUATION

You have a hostage situation on your hands if you have the following:

1. *Substantive demands:* These are demands directly related to the hostage taking. The hostage taker relates the taking of hostages to the fulfillment of certain conditions that are specified.
2. *A need to live on the part of the hostage taker:* If there is no need to live, you may have a different type of situation, such as a suicidal subject. Consider.
3. *A perceived threat of force shown by the authorities.*
4. *Communication between the hostage taker and the authorities:* Remember that communication can take many forms. Be alert for it.

5. *A leader among the hostage takers:* Without a leader, you may have chaos and great difficulty negotiating an agreement. Always try to find a leader among the subjects.
6. *Containment in the smallest possible area:* Why should they negotiate with us at all if they can come and go as they please or move freely about their stronghold?
7. *A negotiator that represents the authorities,* and yet continually expresses, both by word and deed, that he or she is willing to help.
8. *Time:* In a hostage situation, the longer the situation goes, the greater the likelihood that it will end successfully. The longer a situation goes in which no deaths occur, the greater the likelihood is that no deaths will occur. In a crisis situation, for example a barricaded suicidal person, time may work against us. Timely contact is often imperative. Do not confuse the two issues.

REVIEW THE BASIC STEPS FOR CONTACT WITH THE HOSTAGE TAKER

- Prepare your opening statement.
- Ask the subject to come out early in the conversation.
- If the subject will not come out early, ask again later.
- Ignore the hostages, if you can.
- Use cover, if needed.
- Do not tell the subject "no."
- Do not volunteer information to the subject.
- Let the subject talk about whatever he or she wants to talk about.
- If at a loss for words, repeat the subject's last statement or use the "pat" phrases.
- Make the subject feel that he or she is important to you.
- Note the subject's demands. Write them down. Do not trivialize them.
- Use the subject's first name, if appropriate. Ask permission if you are not sure.
- Let the subject talk. Try not to cut the subject off when he or she is speaking.
- Listen carefully to what the subject says.

- Never make promises that you cannot keep or do not intend to keep.
- Do not evaluate the stated beliefs of the subject. That is the way he or she sees things.
- Let the subject know that you are trying to understand his or her point of view.
- Accepting the subject's point of view is not the same as agreeing with it.
- Make the subject work for whatever he or she gets.

USE BOARDS

Keeping track of what is going on, what has gone on, during negotiations is an important function of a negotiations team. Because situations may continue for a long time, the ability to call up historical information may aid in the development of current plans and actions. The size of the team and the size of the scenario will often be a determining factor in how elaborate these information "boards" should be. Regardless, the information is valuable. Records that are developed and maintained effectively will be of greater value to the negotiator and all involved. Often these records are maintained by a negotiator working in the intelligence area of the negotiations command post. They can also be maintained in the negotiations area depending on the needs of the team and of the incident.

Chronological—a complete record of the incident times and actions taken

Positive police actions—what the police have done for the hostage taker

Demands—substantive demands made by the subject

Concessions—concessions made by police to the subject

Weapons—possessed by the subject

Surrender plan—developed by SWAT and negotiators to avoid problems at resolution

Weather—current weather at the incident site and relevant forecasts

Time check—correct time

Profile board—all information related to a specific hostage or hostage taker; one board per person

Lies—lies told by the police
Personnel—a listing of all police and related personnel working or scheduled to work the current incident
Maps and plans
Things "we" want to know
Ready reference
Tactical points
Sickness monitoring
Discussion points—or demands

IGNORE DEADLINES, BUT BE PREPARED TO EXPLAIN

Although deadlines can be difficult to deal with, and offer some uncertainty, in these situations, few people die when deadlines are not met. It can happen, but because hostage situations do not occur in a vacuum, there are real considerations for the hostage taker who kills a hostage. Hostages are taken, and are needed, as shields and as ways of pushing out against the authorities. Without the hostages taken, the taker reduces his or her negotiating power and the shield. Deadlines should be considered within this context. The totality of the situation will help determine the seriousness of a given deadline. In addition, if hostages begin to die by the hand of the hostage taker, usually negotiations will cease and the situation will become tactical. It may even be necessary to remind the subject of this at appropriate times.

1. Do not be overly concerned about deadlines. Understand them within the context of the situation at the time that the deadline is set.
2. The negotiator should be sure that he or she is on the phone or in contact with the subject as the deadline passes.
3. As the deadline passes, talk to the subject about things other than the deadline.
4. Talk the subject through the deadline by talking around it in some way. Bring up other areas of discussion.
5. Do not remind the subject that the deadline has passed.
6. If you can, make excuses about why the deadline cannot be met. Blame the problems on someone else (e.g., administration, the world situation, etc.).

7. Use the phrase, "I'm working on it," as needed.
8. Do not represent to the hostage taker that you think that a deadline is a "big deal."
9. The way in which you approach the hostage taker may encourage the subject to suspend his or her disbelief about the outcome of the incident. Your approach may focus the subject on the possibilities of getting what he or she needs just long enough for you to be able to achieve a successful resolution.
10. Help the subject to see that what happens is really up to him or her and that you will help if the subject will let you.

LISTEN FOR DEMANDS

1. Give yourself plenty of room to negotiate.
2. Start by asking for a lot. This gives you fall back positions from which to work when the subject refuses.
3. Make the subject work for everything that is asked for. This creates problems for the subject to solve and tends to reduce expectations.
4. Use every decision made or concession anticipated to keep the subject occupied and working.
5. In a hostage situation, always try to get something in return for every concession made. In crisis situations, this is not necessary.
6. Conserve concessions as long as possible.
7. Do not concede too fast.
8. Some concessions may get promises only.
9. Be careful about conceding on good faith or to establish rapport. In crisis situations, no problem.
10. Keep a log of all concessions.
11. Never ask for demands. Listen for them.
12. Remember that substantive demands are part of a hostage situation. Nonsubstantive demands may not indicate that you are dealing with a hostage situation.
13. Do not bring up old demands. The subject may lose interest in some demands made as time and negotiations advance.
14. Avoid offering anything.
15. Concessions need not always be tangible.

PREPARE FOR FACE-TO-FACE NEGOTIATIONS

Face-to-face negotiations have a very specific meaning for the hostage and crisis negotiations. The prospect of actually being caught out in the open with an armed hostage taker and hostage is a possibility, but the meaning here is quite different. In the open, you rely on all of your skills and do the best that you can. The consideration of whether or not to go face to face with a hostage taker requires special consideration of several factors.

1. Postpone going face to face until sufficient time has passed to allow for rapport to be built on the phone and for exaggerated emotions to subside. Although there is no specific time requirement, one to two hours after the advent of negotiations is a good starting point.
2. Have adequate cover. Concealment is not enough.
3. Plan a retreat route.
4. Go face to face only with adequate and/or appropriate tactical support.
5. Wear your body armor.
6. Take your weapon and ammunition.
7. Have a physical description of the subject.
8. Give the subject your description. Avoid the possibility of any surprises.
9. Consider whether or not the subject is using this opportunity as a ploy or has a hidden agenda.
10. Review body space concerns and precautions for various types of hostage takers and crisis victims.
11. Maintain eye contact with the subject. His or her eyes may forecast his or her intentions.
12. Face-to-face contacts should be done one-on-one only. Do not go face to face with multiple subjects.
13. Do not attempt this type of negotiations with weapons pointed at you.
14. Never turn your back on the subject.
15. Solicit a definite promise from the subject that, if you go face to face with him or her, the subject will not harm you in any way. If the promise is a definite one, it may increase the probability that the subject will attempt no harm during the negotiations. But it's a probability only; there are no guarantees.

16. If your gut says no, don't go. If everything seems okay, but your internal sensing mechanisms seem uncertain or hesitant, avoid the face-to-face encounter until you can determine the cause of the uncertainty or hesitancy.

SET GOALS FOR NEGOTIATIONS

Our goal as crisis interveners and hostage negotiators is to save lives. This includes all of the parties to the incident. It includes good guys, bad guys, bystanders, hostages, and anyone else affected. Life is the issue, and saving it is our guiding principle.

1. If you can negotiate, then negotiate.
2. Do not be too quick to conclude that negotiating is not possible. Keep trying.
3. In deciding to negotiate, liability issues are always present. Maybe that is a good reason to record all negotiations.
4. Only negotiate for as long as a life is worth.
5. Hostage and crisis negotiating is not a "wait and see" option.
6. Negotiating is an intensive, highly skilled dimension of police work.
7. Success rates in hostage and crisis negotiations are extremely high nationwide.
8. Strive to know when negotiations will not work. Do not jump to this conclusion; evaluate your situation.
9. When asked if negotiations are working, be prepared to provide informed and educated answers. Some believe that a negotiator will argue to continue negotiating even if there is little to support his or her position. Most negotiators are not trained this way. It is important that you know your craft very well and are able to convey that you know what you are talking about.
10. Recognize that negotiations and crisis intervention are tools. Tactical responses are tools also. Avoid seeing negotiators and SWAT as antagonistic. See each as tools that must be used separately or together at certain times to accomplish the overall goal. Using SWAT is not a failure for negotiators. Resolving a situation through negotiation is not a failure for SWAT. It takes both to get the job done.

REMEMBER THAT NEGOTIATIONS ARE A TEAM EFFORT

1. Take your time and work together.
2. Remember that you are working as a team.
3. Utilize all aspects of your team organization. Use the secondary negotiator, intelligence coordinator, think tank, coach, and others as needed and as assigned.
4. Support one another. Learn how to win together and to lose together.
5. Use time between contacts with the subject to update information, generate fresh ideas, and plan and set goals.
6. Be involved in the problem, but avoid being part of the problem or overwhelmed by it.
7. Take care of one another. This is not a "filler" or not "cop like." Do it.
8. Never trade weapons, drugs, people, release of prisoners, or alcohol. If any exceptions to guidelines are to be considered, do it as a team.
9. Never trivialize a demand.
10. Evaluate each demand for the needs expressed.
11. Search for reasons behind behavior.
12. Look for acceptable compromises.
13. Analyze every problem presented or determined.
14. Do not expect that the subject will be willing to give you all of the information that you need to know.
15. Look for the relationships that may exist between the hostage taker and the hostages. Consider relationships that may have existed preincident.
16. Document the entire scenario. Keep accurate and up-to-date records of everything that happens. Record what you do. Record what the subject and the hostages do. Write things down. You will not be able to remember all of the important details. This is important during the incident and may be important afterward.
17. Make sure that all members of the team are managing their own experiences during the scenario and have what they need to sustain themselves.

KEEP THE SUBJECT IN PROBLEM-SOLVING MODE

Helping the subject to solve his or her problems may be one of the most important parts of the overall negotiations effort.

1. Imagine yourself in the other person's situation.
2. Do not assume that you know the subject's intentions.
3. Try to determine the degree to which your own biases are affecting your ability to understand the issues of the subject.
4. Do not blame the subject for his or her inability to cope.
5. Do not blame the subject for your issues.
6. Discuss each other's perceptions.
7. Look for opportunities to act in ways that may be inconsistent with the way in which the subject sees you.
8. Give the subject opportunities to be part of the solution to the present situation. Show how the subject has a stake in the outcome, both immediate and in his or her future.
9. Acknowledge the subject's emotions.
10. Refrain from reacting to emotional outbursts.
11. If you first take time to understand the subject, he or she then may be able to better understand you and what is necessary to manage the situation.
12. Be concerned about the subject's needs and interests. It is a powerful tool.
13. Remember that both sides will have multiple interests and that many of them will differ.
14. Strive to find common interests and then use them to the maximum extent possible.
15. Be concerned with trying to meet the needs of the subject. Whether or not you are actually able to meet those needs, the subject should always believe that you are trying to help in that regard.

DETERMINE WHETHER YOU ARE MAKING PROGRESS

Guessing is not an option. Neither is failure. One will get you the other. If you guess, you fail. Knowing if you are actually making progress is vital. It is vital for the negotiator, and it provides the basis for justifying your work to those who may question it. If you know whether or not you are being successful, you will also know if your chosen direction must continue or if other tools are necessary for success.

Progress is probably being made if the following occurs:

1. There has been no recent loss of life. In this case, loss of life prior to the commencement of negotiations is generally not considered. Loss of life subsequent to negotiations is an important indicator.
2. The hostage taker is talking more than before.
3. The content of the hostage taker's conversations is now less violent in nature.
4. Speech patterns change. Voice pitch lowers. Calmer tones are heard. The speech is slower.
5. The subject is willing to discuss personal matters.
6. At those times that the negotiator takes a "time-out," and gets off of the phone, the hostage taker does not want the negotiator to leave.
7. The subject seems to become more rational than before.
8. There is a reduction in violent behavior.

KNOW HOW TO USE PAT WORDS AND PHRASES

When you may not know what to say next, this is the place to look. Following is a list of several words and phrases that have little or no emotional load associated with them. They are nonjudgmental, and encourage talking and deal with feelings. Used properly when you do not know where to go next, they will give you time to think and will demonstrate your ongoing interest in the subject and his or her problems. Use them individually and judiciously for best results. At times, all of us are at a loss for words. These pat words and phrases have been tested repeatedly, and they will help you get going again.

- "First, I'd like to get to know you better."
- "Could you tell me about it?"
- "I would like to hear your side."

- "Could you share that with me?"
- "I guess that's pretty important to you."
- "Tell me about it."
- "That's interesting."
- "I see."
- "Is that so?"
- "Oh."
- "Uh-huh." (Bolz and Schlossberg, 1982, p. 42. Used with permission.)

You may find that a well-placed grunt will do wonders for your communication skills.

GO STEP BY STEP

1. Preplan.
2. Receive notification.
3. Ask questions.

- Team
- Equipment
- Who, what, where, when, why, and how

4. Slow down.
5. Prepare self.

- Personal
- Check equipment
- Check team equipment
- Check enroute

6. Ascertain best way in.
7. Arrive at assembly point or arrive at scene.
8. Proceed to command post.
9. Brief with incident commander.
10. Assemble with negotiations team.

- Slow everything down
- Establish negotiating area
- Brief with team

11. Determine positions.

   - Primary negotiator (#1)
   - Secondary negotiator (#2)
   - Coach/police psychologist (#3)
   - Intelligence coordinator (#4)
   - Negotiations team leader (#5)

12. Set up equipment.
13. Go through checklists.
14. Gather initial intelligence.
15. Interview first-response officer.
16. Interview others.
17. Meet with tactical commander.
18. Meet with on-scene commander.
19. Attempt to make initial contact.
20. Cut off phone service.
21. Put in hostage phone.
22. Continue evaluation of situation.
23. Determine status of utilities.
24. Think "intelligence."
25. Maintain logs.
26. Continue to establish rapport.
27. Ask hostage taker to come out.
28. Begin to negotiate.
29. Establish "we-they."

   - Gather intelligence
   - Maintain intelligence boards

30. Ignore the hostages.
31. Take time-outs.
32. Discuss and evaluate with team.
33. Take care of yourself.
34. Avoid deadlines.
35. Talk through deadlines.
36. Avoid face-to-face negotiations.
37. Attempt face-to-face carefully.

   - Cover
   - Weapon

- Tactical back-up
- Retreat route
- Promise from hostage taker
- Protective vest
- Wait a reasonable time before attempting
- If your gut says no, don't go

38. Make concessions slowly.
39. Do not trivialize demands.
40. Get something in return for all concessions in hostage situations (not applicable in crisis situations).
41. Be an agent of reality.
42. Avoid lying.
43. If you must lie, lie only about large things, never about small things.
44. Allow ventilation.
45. Don't take verbal abuse personally.
46. Give due credit to the hostage taker.
47. Pass the buck.
48. Delay, delay, delay.
49. Empathize with the hostages.
50. Pass intelligence.
51. Receive intelligence.
52. Establish diagnosis.
53. Meet with negotiations team.
54. Determine negotiations strategies.
55. Pass intelligence to the tactical team.
56. Change negotiator, if necessary.
57. Encourage surrender.
58. Avoid "bullet words."
59. Communicate effectively and actively.
60. Plan surrender carefully.
61. Meet concerns about surrender.
62. Work out surrender details with hostage taker.
63. Work out surrender details with tactical unit.
64. Review surrender plans with hostage taker prior to initiation.
65. Proceed carefully with surrender.
66. Debrief hostages or victims.
67. Debrief hostage taker.
68. Provide medical and psychological assistance.

69. Reassemble team equipment.
70. Keep promises.
71. Debrief hostage negotiations team immediately after incident.
72. Debrief with tactical unit separately.
73. Safeguard tape recordings of negotiations.
74. Safeguard logs of negotiations.
75. Complete incident reports.
76. Add the following wherever and whenever appropriate:

  * Keep the tactical commander advised.
  * Keep the incident commander advised.
  * Give time for the hostage taker to calm down.
  * Plan personal equipment.
  * Avoid the negative effects of time.
  * Bargain for everything in a hostage situation (not so with a crisis situation).
  * Separate people from problems.
  * Look for interests.
  * Determine alternatives.
  * Be legitimate.
  * Know the law.
  * Don't moralize.
  * Support one another.
  * Listen carefully.
  * Keep yourself under control.

UNDERSTAND AND USE STOCKHOLM SYNDROME

The history of Stockholm syndrome is omitted purposely here. Research into the background of this phenomenon is left to the reader. It should be noted that some scholars question the existence of Stockholm syndrome. However, because it has been observed to occur in hostage situations, this author feels that it is important to detail what happens and how it can be used to our advantage, and to protect the hostages.

Stockholm syndrome develops as a result of human bonding that occurs under severe traumatic conditions and over a period of time, such as hostage takings. It does not occur in nontraumatic situations. For instance, some have implied that this syndrome could occur between the hostage taker and the negotiator after long periods of negotiations. This is not the case. Although other types of bonding may occur here, the negotiator is not trapped in a traumatic situation with the hostage taker. His or her life is not in danger and the hostage taker has no control over the negotiator. This syndrome must be understood in terms of this traumatic bonding in order to make sense to negotiators who must learn to use its results.

1. Stockholm syndrome is an automatic, unconscious, and emotional response to the trauma of being taken hostage.
2. The resulting survival skills that emerge are not the same as conscious coping skills that are learned in a classroom or through experience. These survival skills are manifest at an unconscious level.
3. The bond that is formed is a positive bond between the hostage taker and the hostages even though it is formed during a traumatic and dangerous time. The fact that the threats may be that of bodily harm or death, the bonding is a positive one rather than being negative. An example might be that the hostage, although threatened with death, will see the hostage taker as benevolent for not taking his or her life. Because the hostage taker is seen as giving the hostage his or her life, by not taking it, the hostage may feel positively toward the taker.
4. As the positive feelings are developed from hostage to hostage taker, the hostage taker may develop positive feelings toward the hostage.
5. To the degree that positive feelings begin to develop in this way, the hostage taker may be less likely to actually harm the hostage.
6. The downside to the development of this syndrome is that, even with the positive feelings between taker and hostage, there may be very negative feelings from the hostage toward the authorities. This should be anticipated and plans should be formulated to handle this eventuality. This is especially important during the surrender process when the hostage can turn against those who are actually there to rescue him or her.
7. Remember, the reactions of the hostage are internal mechanisms designed by nature to foster survival at a very basic level.

8. Stockholm syndrome can be enhanced by the negotiator in certain ways.

   • When food is bargained for, send in unprepared food rather than that which requires no preparation. This will encourage bonding because all involved must work together to prepare the food to be eaten.
   • Encourage the hostage taker to take responsibility for the well-being and for the medical problems of the hostage. Especially encourage attention to those who must take medication regularly or who must be attended to routinely for particular problems. Try to place the responsibility for caring for these individuals on the shoulders of the hostage taker. It is harder to harm someone to whom you are ministering.

9. Learn to understand Stockholm syndrome so that if it does occur, you will be prepared to use it to your advantage.
10. Stockholm syndrome will usually not develop with certain types of hostage takers and hostage situations. These situations include domestic crisis situations and those involving psychopathic hostage takers.
11. The amount of time needed to develop this syndrome varies from situation to situation. In some cases, it will develop very quickly. In others, much more slowly over many hours or days. This author has seen it develop in training simulations. Because it is unconscious, emotional, and automatic in humans, it is particularly powerful and significant. It occurs when a person is threatened, and because of that threat, the survival mode is activated.

THE DOS AND DON'TS FOR HOSTAGE AND CRISIS NEGOTIATORS

The Dos

• Have a good opening statement.
• Be empathetic.
• Be credible.

- Have good voice control.
- Develop tolerance for stress.
- Gather intelligence.
- Put together a psychological profile.
- Listen actively.
- Pause periodically.
- Encourage ventilation on the part of the subject.
- Utilize self-disclosure very carefully.
- Be flexible.
- Nurture the escape potential.
- Use open-ended questions.
- Be reassuring.
- Make the subject feel responsible for the hostages or victims.
- List demands accurately.
- Pass off personal responsibility when talking to the subject.
- Talk in terms of "we," with the "we" meaning the subject and negotiator.
- Talk on the subject's intellectual level.
- Use reflection techniques as a way of letting the subject know that you are listening.
- Acknowledge the subject's feelings.
- Use reassuring remarks and clichés.
- Give positive approval.
- Keep the subject in a decision-making mode.

The Don'ts

- Interrupt the subject.
- Ask superfluous questions.
- Be argumentative.
- Insert anything for "what it's worth."
- Make decisions.
- Make promises.
- Use "trigger" words.
- Say "we" meaning negotiator and police.
- Get the subject irritated.
- Volunteer information.
- Talk too much.
- Get mad or irritated.

- Make assumptions.
- Be authoritarian.
- Be tough unless it is needed and appropriate.
- Be soft unless appropriate.
- Be defensive.

USE TIME APPROPRIATELY

Time is generally thought of as an ally of the hostage negotiator. The longer negotiations go, the better. The longer things go without injury or loss of life, the greater the probability that no life will be lost. The more time used in such a situation, the greater the probability that a successful resolution will be realized. This may well be true for negotiations when you have a true hostage situation. For those situations that are not defined hostage situations, time may not be helpful. Situations involving suicidal, barricaded, or domestic crises usually require a somewhat quicker response. These are not hostage situations and require crisis intervention for successful management. The key to knowing about the advantages of time in a particular situation is based on your knowledge and evaluation of whether or not the incident before you is a hostage situation or a crisis.

1. Time is the ally of the negotiator in a hostage situation.
2. Time may not be an ally in a crisis situation.
3. Time allows the negotiator to work on strategy.
4. Time allows for the increase in basic human needs, the satisfying of which can be used as a negotiating tactic.
5. Time allows for rapport to be established between the subject and the negotiator.
6. Time allows the development of a dependent relationship of the subject to the negotiator.
7. Time allows for anxiety to be reduced.
8. Time allows for rational thought to increase.
9. Time allows for human bonding to occur between the hostage taker and the hostages. This is referred to as Stockholm syndrome.
10. Time increases opportunities for the hostages to escape.
11. Time allows for better decision making on both sides.

12. Time allows for hostage taker expectations to be reduced.
13. Time brings on exhaustion. This is good for the subject to experience; bad for the negotiator.
14. Time may create a loss of objectivity on both sides. This is not a good thing for the negotiator.
15. Time increases the onset of boredom.
16. Time may create a "creeping up" effect during which established perimeters begin to collapse and control of the situation may be reduced.

UNDERSTAND WHY WE DO NOT TRADE HOSTAGES

Why should you not trade one hostage for another? Why not send in a volunteer officer to take the place of a young child? Wouldn't that be the noble and brave thing to do? In actuality, the horror stories are abundant when this has been done. Common sense may advocate for such a move, but your trained, uncommon sense must tell you that this should not be done. Why?

1. If the trade involves a police officer that is traded in for a civilian hostage, this may increase the willingness of the hostage taker to kill. Think about it: Killing a civilian is one thing. Being able to say that you killed a police officer is quite another.
2. Introducing a new hostage into a group that has been together in a traumatic venue for a long time may increase the tension in that group. It may make the group uneasy. More important, it may raise the tension for the hostage taker who does not know this new person. Anything that raises tension unnecessarily works to the disadvantage of the authorities and the negotiator.
3. The human bonding process that is dependent on time and the relationships between those held hostage and the hostage taker may be disturbed by putting a new person in the group and removing another. Some refer to this bonding as Stockholm syndrome. Such bonding is a way of safeguarding the hostages, and as such should not be disturbed unless absolutely necessary.
4. If the trading of hostages involves a specific person requested by the hostage taker, the ploy could be establishing an audience for the suicidal gesture of the hostage taker. In the alternative, it

could be a ploy designed for the homicide of the person requested. Careful evaluation of these issues is always important.
5. If this request is made, evaluate the request carefully to gain additional understanding of the mental status and intentions of the hostage taker.

USE TRANSLATORS APPROPRIATELY AND EFFECTIVELY

The method of using a translator during negotiations with a non-English speaking hostage taker or crisis victim is often compromised by lack of proper training for negotiators and by misunderstandings about effective procedure. Translators are of value only if they, or their agency, can be trusted, and if their contribution to the negotiations fosters negotiations team involvement and a successful resolution to the incident. One common mistake is allowing the translator to conduct negotiations. Regardless of the language spoken, and translated, the police negotiator must conduct the actual negotiations with the subject. This is true even if the translator happens to be a trained negotiator.

1. Translators must be chosen carefully prior to an actual incident. If this person can participate in training scenarios, so much the better.
2. Translators should be recruited from reputable agencies that provide such services.
3. In the alternative to an agency, a specific person with the required skills should be sought, evaluated, and trained by the negotiations team.
4. The translator acts as a "word machine" only for the primary negotiator.
5. He or she does not conduct the ongoing negotiations with the subject.
6. Translators musts be able to say to the subject exactly what the negotiator says in the same way as the negotiator says it.
7. Similarly, he or she must be able to say to the primary negotiator exactly what the subject says and in the same way that the subject says it.

8. Translators should not paraphrase what either the negotiator or subject says.
9. Information about the subject's tone, inflection, cultural meanings, etc., will be given directly to the negotiator if such nuances may not successfully cross cultural boundaries. The translator should be instructed to do this by the negotiator.
10. Translators should not add personal interpretations about what the subject or negotiator is saying.
11. The translator should be fluent specifically in English and in the language of the non–English-speaking subject.
12. He or she should have no conflicts of interest that would prevent him or her from relating information accurately or from working with the police in the resolution of the incident. This must be explored before the translator is used.
13. When using the translator, the negotiator should speak in short phrases in order to allow for accurate translation. This takes practice.
14. The translator should translate in short phrases.
15. The translator is not part of the negotiations think tank unless specifically needed.
16. Remember: The translator only translates. Nothing more.

KNOW WHEN AND HOW TO CALL A TIME-OUT

A time-out is a pause in negotiations determined by the negotiator or by the team. A time-out may be taken at any reasonable time, but there are specific times when one would be advisable.

1. When it is necessary to review what has been heard or learned
2. To think of questions to ask
3. To explore alternatives
4. To develop statements that are more persuasive
5. To review strategy and relevant tactics
6. To discuss possible concessions
7. To determine how to react to new demands
8. To consult experts or team advisors
9. To check on departmental policy or to check on specific points of the law

10. To analyze changes in demands, new behaviors, attitudes of the subject, or specific facts
11. To stall questions of the subject that might be embarrassing to the negotiator
12. To change the subject
13. To get rest, food, or fluids for the negotiator
14. To go to the bathroom
15. At any time when you may not know what to do next

SELECT A MENTAL HEALTH PROFESSIONAL TO ASSIST THE TEAM

The selection of a mental health professional to work with a negotiations team is an important decision. All mental health professionals are not trained to work in this environment. In fact, most probably do not want to. Some who may be quite willing will not be effective. One responsibility that accrues to the team is to make a selection that will ultimately be of benefit to the team in the field. The decision tree in Figure 6.1 may be helpful in this regard.

BE A MENTAL HEALTH CONSULTANT TO A NEGOTIATIONS TEAM

The Calls

I have received calls from various parts of the country from psychologists who are being recruited by police departments and sheriff's offices. They are being recruited as mental health consultants for hostage and crisis negotiations teams within these departments. Generally, these psychologists are not full-time police psychologists with a police agency, but rather independent practitioners or employee assistance professionals. They are flattered by the invitation to be a part of a police unit and drawn by the potential for additional training and the anticipated excitement of the incidents.

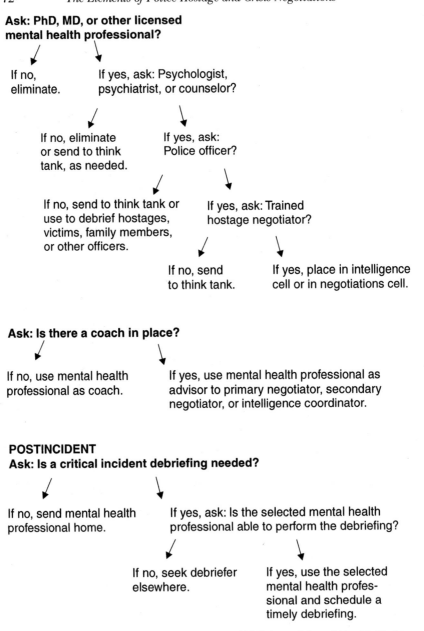

Ask: PhD, MD, or other licensed mental health professional?

If no, eliminate.

If yes, ask: Psychologist, psychiatrist, or counselor?

If no, eliminate or send to think tank, as needed.

If yes, ask: Police officer?

If no, send to think tank or use to debrief hostages, victims, family members, or other officers.

If yes, ask: Trained hostage negotiator?

If no, send to think tank.

If yes, place in intelligence cell or in negotiations cell.

Ask: Is there a coach in place?

If no, use mental health professional as coach.

If yes, use mental health professional as advisor to primary negotiator, secondary negotiator, or intelligence coordinator.

POSTINCIDENT
Ask: Is a critical incident debriefing needed?

If no, send mental health professional home.

If yes, ask: Is the selected mental health professional able to perform the debriefing?

If no, seek debriefer elsewhere.

If yes, use the selected mental health professional and schedule a timely debriefing.

FIGURE 6.1. Decision Tree for Selecting and Utilizing a Mental Health Professional to Assist the Negotiations Team

The Background

Most of the callers have had little or no experience with police negotiations teams. Some had no experience with the police at all. Some have been involved with the police only to the extent that they may have administered psychological evaluations to potential police candidates. None were police officers themselves, either past, present. or reserve.

The Questions

Their questions were many and varied. They included:

1. What do I do?
2. What are my obligations to the team?
3. What about my liability exposure?
4. Do I need special liability insurance to cover me during my work on an incident?
5. What about time commitments?
6. What if I am called at 2:00 in the morning?
7. How can I respond to a team callout if I am a single parent?
8. How much training will I need to do this job?
9. How much time should I allow?
10. How involved should I become?
11. How much should I charge for my services to the hostage and crisis negotiations team?
12. Should I become a police officer or a reserve police officer?
13. Should I contract for a flat fee to cover my services?
14. Should I volunteer my time?
15. How much time should I give to the team?
16. Can I limit my involvement with the team?
17. Do I need to be there for the team every time they call on me?
18. How do I get the training that I need to do this job?
19. Should I get involved with the negotiations team at all? Is this for me?
20. What will my role be during an actual incident?
21. Will the negotiators take me seriously if I'm not a sworn officer?

The Quandary: Love It or Leave It

These questions, and others, formed the basis for most of the calls. Certainly, I did not know all of the answers to all of the questions. Neither could I know the particulars of each individual circumstance. I did know, however, that being involved with a police hostage and crisis negotiations team fell into one of two categories: either you loved doing it even with all of its inconveniences, or you hated the idea and wanted nothing of it. There does not seem to be a middle ground. I suppose that if individuals involved themselves to the point of providing periodic training for the team, and nothing else, that that could constitute a middle ground. However, it does not amount to the involvement requested and needed by most hostage negotiations teams. Colleagues of mine, who do this type of work on a full-time basis, and/or who are employed primarily by a law enforcement agency, would not do anything else. They love the involvement and the challenge. They are constantly involved with their team and the team is constantly involved with them. My experience has been that most nonpolice psychologists and other mental health professionals are initially drawn by the excitement of crisis incidents that they are usually not involved in, but do not want the ongoing responsibility that comes with active membership on a team as the mental health consultant. At meetings that I have attended of police psychologists, many, perhaps even most, with whom I have spoken, love the psychological services aspects of working with a police agency. However, they want nothing to do with the police aspects, especially those involving hostage and crisis negotiations.

How to Respond

So, how should I respond to their inquiries? What should I tell them to do, if anything at all? What about special issues peculiar to specific jurisdictions? Where should I refer them? How do I get them to look inward and recognize their real interests and true needs rather than getting involved just because they were asked? And, what happens if they accept an invitation from a negotiations team and then, after realizing what is required, they cannot fulfill the commitment that they have made? What about the team and their needs? The business of hostage and crisis negotiations is imminently serious business. Unlike the private or institutional mental health practice, hostage and crisis situations require continuous and pinpoint accuracy often over an extended period of time and usually under less than ideal circumstances. A psychologist's commitment and involvement with such a team must take this into account. Clearly, this is not a job for everyone. But, most jobs are not for everyone. If you are going to do the job, however, it is important to gain a well-grounded understanding of the part that you will need to play in the overall scenario. To do less than that lets everybody down, yourself included. To do less may also tarnish the image of psychology in general, and police psychology in particular.

The Responses

What Do I Do?

First, talk to the person who invited you to work with the team. What did this person have in mind for you? If this person is not the negotiations team leader, how does the team leader feel about your involvement and what does this person see as your role? What about training for you in hostage and crisis negotiations? How will that be provided? One of my callers said that he had already been to training and because of it, had a better idea of what negotiators did and how he might be part of the process. Sometimes, it is very difficult to get into police negotiations training programs if you are not a police officer or a police psychologist who works with a negotiations team. Up-front training may offer some valuable insights that will be useful in making your decision to become involved.

What Are My Obligations to the Team?

Obligations to the team will probably be directly related to your agreed-upon involvement. My opinion is that if you are going to become involved in this way that you have a major obligation to the negotiations team and its members to be there for them and the team as a whole whenever they need you. If that is too much, adjust accordingly. Just be clear with the team to avoid misunderstandings and bad feelings on both sides. Without such an understanding, your credibility as a mental health consultant could be in jeopardy.

What About My Liability Exposure?

I do not know the exact answer to this question. If you are full time with a department and functioning as the police psychologist and your job description indicates that consulting to the negotiations team is part of the territory, you are probably okay. Even this may not be one hundred percent true in our litigious society. Part-time people probably pose a different problem. Check with your liability insurance carrier. Is this new involvement considered within the purview of your work as a psychologist or other mental health professional? Licensing boards may be helpful also. Approach this area with care, but be careful not to catastrophize either.

Do I Need Special Liability Insurance to Cover Me During My Work on an Incident?

I do not know why you would. However, check the rules in your jurisdiction and also with your insurance carrier. This area of police work is just finding its way into the mental health field as an area of expertise. You may be clearing new ground.

What About Time Commitments?

This can be a problem if you do not think this through and do not understand what your role is on the negotiations team. If the team believes that they can depend on you being there when they need you, then you must be there when they need you. It is just that simple. Simplicity, however, begins to fade very quickly if you do not understand this concept from the outset. You can define your own time commitments to the team, but any reasonable degree of involvement will require much time spent on your part. A negotiations team will look to you for training, planning, assistance at actual incidents, development of training scenarios, postincident debriefings, and a myriad of other tasks both personal and professional. As they develop trust in you, they will come to have greater reliance on you as the needs arise. If you are married, or want to be for a reasonable period of time, you may want to be sure that your significant other really understands what you are getting into. It will not always be convenient for your partner either. Even though you have just spent several hundred dollars for theater tickets and just as the curtain goes up, you are called to a jumper who is all the way across town, you will need to respond. And that's the long and the short of it.

What if I Am Called at 2:00 in the Morning?

And you will be called at 2:00 a.m. or at any time for that matter. My experience is that the callout comes at the most inconvenient times and at those times when I have just finished an entire workday and am tired. It really does not matter. When called, you go. And when you go, nobody cares that you have had a long day and that you would rather be home sleeping. The expectation is that you will be as sharp as you need to be and that you have taken care of your personal needs yourself. You should show up at the scene ready to go to work at whatever task is necessary to support the team effort. This could include hauling equipment or cable, helping with installations, etc., as well as providing professional assistance and backup.

How Can I Respond to a Team Callout
if I Am a Single Parent?

Problem! Obviously, you need an on-call babysitter. If this is a major problem area, it may be necessary to limit your involvement with the team for the benefit of all concerned.

How Much Training Will I Need to Do This Job?

Some states mandate the amount of training that is necessary (Texas Penal Code 16.02). A minimum of forty hours of training in a course that requires practical applications as a part of course of instruction is a must. Retraining should occur annually. Training in related areas would also be helpful. I know of only one course that is offered for police psychologists who are working with hostage teams. It is called, "Hostage Negotiations for Police Psychologists" (North Central Texas Council of Governments Regional Police Academy, Arlington, Texas). Combining your professional training with the specific police hostage negotiations training should be sufficient for novices to this field. Continual training both within and without the team is critical. The team will depend on you to have the best available information in all related areas at your disposal.

How Much Time Should I Allow?

As much time as it takes if you are serious about your involvement.

How Involved Should I Become?

Of course, this is a personal matter. Those of us that are involved probably would get more involved if we could. You may find that this is true for the negotiators also. As I mentioned earlier, either it is for you or it is not for you. If you find your niche, you may find that you want to explore and to develop it to the fullest. Hostage and crisis negotiations teams are often betwixt and between within the departmental structure. Some departments see their negotiations team as a phantom unit that springs to life only when needed, but that otherwise is largely disregarded in the overall scheme of things. Their involvement with each other and with you is important for morale and overall team effectiveness.

How Much Should I Charge for My Services to the Hostage and Crisis Negotiations Team?

If your involvement is part of your job description, no problem. Coming in from the outside may pose additional problems. You can always try to arrange a deal that pays you your normal hourly rate for the actual number of hours worked with the team in training or at incidents. When I have used a backup psychologist during times when I am out of the country, etc., he bills his usual rate. However, he is only used as back-up and not on a regular or ongoing basis. As a result the expense is minimal, but does provide for such assistance to the team on an as-needed basis.

Another possibility is to contract for a flat rate. You would provide the needed input and services and draw a standard monthly compensation. Of course, this means that you could spend one hour or twenty hours for the same money. There is nothing wrong with this as long as you are clear about it. My reality is that you need to be compensated. However, if the compensation is the sole motivator, perhaps it is time to reconsider your choice.

Should I Become a Police Officer or a Reserve Police Officer?

Now here is an excellent idea, in my opinion. Establish your credibility in this police-specific endeavor by learning to do the job of a police officer from the inside. Usually, reserve officers are not paid for their services, but they are provided with training and equipment. The training is worth its weight in gold to someone who really wants to get involved in this area. In Texas, reserve officers are required to pass through several training levels that eventually result in a regular peace officer license. Most departments do require that reserve officers work for the department a defined number of hours per week or month. The reality is that a psychologist does not have to be a police officer to be an effective member of a hostage and crisis negotiations team. But, it sure helps.

Should I Contract for a Flat Fee to Cover My Services?

Explore this with your department. It may be a more realistic approach all around rather than charging your hourly rate.

Should I Volunteer My Time?

Yes, especially at first. Prove your worth to the team and to the department. It might make it easier to get the money flowing once they see the necessity of having you on board. And, it really is important to give something back. The rewards are not so bad either.

How Much Time Should I Give to the Team?

Give as much time as you want to and as much as you can. The more that they see you and come to rely on your presence, the greater your credibility. Credibility with police officers takes time, but is worth the effort. Do not ever confuse their politeness toward civilians like yourself with credibility. You build credibility by credible involvement.

Can I Limit My Involvement with the Team?

Of course you can limit your involvement with the negotiations team. You may want to start slowly and give more time as you find that you like working in this area. Be clear with the team and with the department about the amount of time that you are willing to give. Don't be shy about it. They may want more from you, but they will appreciate your honesty. You can always increase your time given.

Do I Need to Be There for the Team Every Time They Call on Me?

If you tell the team that you will be there, be there! Most understand occasional illness or if you are out of town. If you have defined a limited role for yourself, this may solve the problem. But if you have signed on for the long haul, they will look for you when something happens. In reality, if you do not show up, nobody will say a word. But it will be quietly understood that they should not depend on you. The implications of this can be great or small according to how you have fashioned your relationship with the team.

How Do I Get the Training That I Need to Do This Job?

Ask for training. Even, insist upon it if you are to become involved. Training comes in various forms and you should take it upon yourself to find out what and where training is available in hostage and crisis negotiations. You may be able to get the department to pay for or to provide your initial training, but be prepared to get the needed training regardless. Training is not uniformly provided across the United States. Each state does it differently. The hostage and crisis negotiations courses offered at various training centers might include the following:

1. Basic Hostage and Crisis Negotiations—40 hours
2. Advanced Hostage and Crisis Negotiations—40 hours
3. Accelerated/Recertification Hostage Negotiations—48 hours. This is a level III course and requires successful completion of the basic and advanced courses.
4. First Responder to Hostage and Crisis Situations—16 hours
5. Hostage Negotiations for Police Psychologists—40 hours
6. The Psychology of Hostage Negotiations—24 hours

You may want to contact various police organizations such as the International Association of Chiefs of Police and get their training catalog. In more and more states and regions, professional organizations of hostage and crisis negotiators are being formed. Some have existed for many years and have developed their own in-house basic training programs. You may want to affiliate with the group in your area.

Should I Get Involved with the Negotiations Team at All? Is This for Me?

This should be your first question. This work is not for everybody. Talk to the team. Talk to others in our field who have become involved. See what they think. What problems have they encountered? Carefully consider your motives for considering this line of work in addition to your full-time job. Can you do it in a way that compliments what you are now doing? Does it feel right? You probably already know the answer to this question.

What Will My Role Be During an Actual Incident?

When you go to training, most of these types of questions will be answered. It will become obvious to you where you will fit in the overall scheme. Talking with other police psychologists who are involved with a team will help define your role. Even asking your team what role they might want you to play during an incident might be helpful. Normally, the role of the police psychologist or mental health consultant is to assist the negotiators in profiling hostage takers and victims, and then helping to formulate negotiations strategies. You may also be involved in the negotiations room with the primary and secondary negotiators. You provide an extra set of eyes and ears during the negotiations. You also provide encouragement and stress management for the negotiators. Conceivably, you might be involved in intelligence gathering, talking with medical and psychiatric personnel about the subject, setting up equipment, updating the situation logs, or consulting with the special weapons and tactics team commander about courses of action. You may find yourself operating completely in the negotiations command post or moving between the negotiations unit and the incident command post. As with things of this nature, flexibility and adaptability are the key. Often, you are expected to know more than you, or any other psychologist for that matter, may know. It becomes an opportunity to pull together everything you were ever taught or trained to do and to put it all on the line at a moment's notice. The possibilities are endless.

Will the Negotiators Take Me Seriously if I Am Not a Sworn Officer?

That really depends on you. If you are not credible, it doesn't matter if you are sworn or not. If you do not have the background, training, and involvement with the team, you may not be viewed as serious, and hence not taken seriously. The fact that you may be a former officer or a current reserve officer, with your current department or with another department, establishes that you may know police work. If, however, your professional background, professional and hostage negotiations training, and a firm commitment to the team are not in place, your sworn status will probably do you little good. It all fits together to the benefit of the team and you if you make sure that all the parts are present and properly represented.

Now What?

I am sure you know that when it is all said and done, it is really your decision whether or not to become involved. It is an important decision, to say the least. At the most, your involvement may give you the experience of a lifetime, both personally and professionally.

You will make the correct decision for you. If it does not feel to you like your involvement is the right thing to do, it probably is not regardless of all of the other reasons in the "plus" column. Examine all that is involved and in the last analysis, let your personal energy guide you. In my experience, this energy is very seldom wrong.

Chapter 7

Preparing for the Surrender

UNDERSTAND AND DEVELOP THE PROCESS

This particular part of the response to hostage and barricaded situations is often given only cursory importance in the overall process. Although different teams and different societies handle differently the surrender of those involved, the surrender must be handled effectively. Negotiations or interventions that may have gone extremely well up to the point of surrender, may be lost if this final area is not taken seriously. Some procedures provide for a surrender plan to be in writing and presented at the beginning of an incident. Others are developed only after the subject has agreed to come out. Still other surrenders are handled on a hit-and-miss basis. The goal of most negotiations is to get the perpetrator to come out. Yet, the time given to planning and preparing for this to happen may be underestimated and inadequate.

USE THE GUIDELINES

The following is provided as a guide to the process of subject surrender. It is intended to be a reminder of the importance of this part of the overall process.

1. The surrender process should be coordinated between SWAT and negotiators.
2. When speaking with the subject, maintain a positive attitude about coming out.
3. Talk about "when" the subject comes out rather than about "if" the subject comes out.

4. When anticipating the surrender, do not put hostage phone or other equipment away prematurely. A promised surrender may not occur. You may need your equipment again. Do not be caught unprepared.

5. Be sure to ask for the surrender early in the negotiations. Sometimes the subject will comply. If he or she does not, move on with the negotiations process and ask again later.

6. Do not ask for surrender over and over again. Move on and come back to it.

7. Clearly explain the surrender process to the subject.

8. Do not give confusing instructions or information. Keep it simple.

9. Avoid talking too much about the surrender. It may reflect your own anxiety.

10. If the taker is reluctant to come out, ask him or her to explain his or her reluctance.

11. Problem-solve with the subject if necessary.

12. After working through expressed problems, return to the process.

13. Confirm with the subject that he or she understands what he or she is to do.

14. Explain to the subject what the authorities will do.

15. Clarify with all concerned from where the subject will emerge.

16. Get a promise from the taker that no one will be hurt during the surrender.

17. Take the surrender process seriously.

18. Remember that many hostage takers and barricaded persons will have a need to "surrender with dignity."

19. Allow a dignified surrender if possible.

20. Be alert for a surrender that may result in suicide.

21. If you suspect a suicide attempt instead of the promised surrender, do not let the person off of the phone. Evaluate carefully.

22. Explain to the subject that although the negotiator may be arranging the surrender, instructions will be given by other police officers when the subject emerges.

23. Refer to those who will receive the subject as "police officers" or "deputies," etc., rather than as "SWAT officers" or "tactical officers."

24. Enlist the subject's help in determining the surrender process.
25. Compliment the subject for any help that he or she may give.
26. Deal specifically with the issue of how weapons are to be handled. Will they be left inside the stronghold or tossed out?
27. Be sure that your surrender plan takes into account how hostages or victims will be handled and when and how they should come out.
28. Prior to final implementation, check one last time with all concerned to be sure that the plan is intact both inside and outside the stronghold.
29. If possible, after the surrender, speak with the subject. Find out what happened and what motivated what he or she did and how. What held up an earlier surrender? This information can be useful the next time and can be related to future negotiator training.
30. Avoid accepting invitations to have the subject surrender to you individually.
31. If you agree to be available to the subject immediately after the incident is resolved, honor that agreement.
32. If you have made other promises, honor those too.
33. If you must leave the phone at a remote location to be present at the place of the surrender, put another negotiator on the phone with the subject until the surrender is complete.
34. If you use a second negotiator to remain on the phone with the subject, be sure to introduce that negotiator to the subject if at all possible. Explain to the subject what you are doing.
35. Compliment the subject on agreeing to come out because it is "the right thing to do," and that this "is the right time to do it."
36. Deal realistically with police issues such as "handcuffing" and "going to jail."
37. If a particular circumstance exists that may affect the way a surrender is done, or that may have a direct bearing on the willingness to surrender, discuss this with the tactical commander and the on-scene commander before making any commitments. Some of these circumstances may involve religious needs, physical needs, dignity needs, etc.
38. Take seriously all concerns expressed by the subject. Try to resolve them if you can. Explain if you cannot.

39. Differentiate between legitimate concerns that may stand in the way of the surrender process from tactics on the part of the subject designed to stall negotiations or final resolution.
40. Confront hidden agendas as they are discovered. Discuss these issues with team members.

Chapter 8

Postincident Tasks

DEBRIEF THE HOSTAGE NEGOTIATIONS TEAM

Debriefing after an incident should never be an afterthought. My experience tells me that it is often treated in this way. Regardless of outcome, a postincident debriefing for the negotiations team is important and valuable. Debriefings are best done immediately after an incident, or as soon after the incident as possible. There is a tendency to put off the debriefing because the team is tired or has other responsibilities. Do not fall into this trap. How and when you debrief may determine how you will function the next time. Even if a debriefing is done with the SWAT team, negotiators should get together and hold their own. Team leaders and team members must take responsibility for requesting this time together.

A negotiations team debriefing serves at least two purposes:

1. To discuss actual tactics and strategies used to work and to resolve the latest incident.
2. To allow the team to deal with the emotional issues related to the incident.

Even in successful resolutions, there may be emotions, responses, concerns, and suggestions that the team wants to vent. This will be true especially if the incident went badly. It is more difficult to do this in a combined debriefing or one that is primarily tactical in its orientation.

USE THE DEBRIEFING SHEET

The debriefing sheet and other material that follow are intended to assist a team in conducting a postincident debriefing. The debriefing sheet (Box 8.1) is also a valuable tool for maintaining a record of hos-

BOX 8.1. Sample Debriefing Sheet

Name given to hostage/crisis situation:
Service number: Type of situation:
Date of situation:
Location:
Time team called:
#1:   Date of HNT debriefing:
#2:   Date of SWAT debriefing:
#3:
#4:
#5:
Other negotiators:
Suspect(s):
Age, race, sex:
Hostages held:
Hostages released:
Family members held:
Family members released:
Deaths:
Injuries:
Motive:
Time event began:
Time event ended:
Total event time:
Time negotiations began:
Time negotiations ended:
Communication method:
Method of resolution: Diagnosis:
Total negotiating time:
Suspect clothing:
Suspect criminal history:
Suspect weapon capability:
Rounds fired:
Targets:
Primary substantive demands:
Other suspect demands:
Demands met:
SWAT deployment:
Criminal charges:
Disposition:
Plead to:
Sentence received:
Other pertinent information about this incident:

tage negotiations team callouts. It can be modified according to individual team needs.

REVIEW THE TEN MOST SERIOUS ERRORS

For the well-trained law enforcement negotiator, errors are what other people make. Success is often related to the avoidance of these serious errors. It is important to know and understand the ten most serious errors made by negotiators. They are as follows:

1. Failure to choose appropriate person as negotiator. (Choose very carefully based on the totality of the presenting circumstances.)
2. Failure to differentiate between a true hostage situation and a crisis situation. (Which is it? You must know in order to take proper action.)
3. Failure to establish timely and meaningful contact with the hostage taker or crisis victim. (Call when you are ready and have the necessary information that you need. Time may be on our side in a hostage situation, but the reverse may be true with a crisis victim.)
4. Failure to procure and to use appropriate data on the hostage taker and on hostages. (Think intelligence first, second, and last. Gather and evaluate intelligence carefully and intelligently.)
5. Failure to keep the hostage taker in a decision-making status. (Keep him or her problem solving. Create management problems.)
6. Failure to recognize the type of hostage taker or crisis victim. (Who or what do you have?)

   - Criminal
   - Person with mental illness
   - Inadequate personality
   - Borderline personality
   - Terrorist
   - Psychopath
   - Someone who is in crisis
   - A person who is suicidal

- A domestic dispute
- Other

7. Failure to recognize the appropriate mind-set of the hostage taker or crisis victim. (Effective profiling is a must. No shotgun approaches, please.)
8. Failure to provide for the safety of the hostage negotiator. (A negotiator in harm's way will not be effective.)
9. Failure to abide by the primary objective of the negotiator. (Our ultimate goal is the preservation of all human life.)
10. Failure to allow sufficient time for negotiations to be effective. (For the hostage negotiator, time is our most important ally. In all situations, how we use time is a critical issue.)

ILLUSTRATIVE CASE STUDY: WHY DID IT WORK?

On April 20, 1998, at 0335, negotiators were deployed to support an officer who was already talking with a subject barricaded in his truck threatening to kill himself. Most of the issues seemed to revolve around family matters.

At 0428, the primary negotiator began to speak directly with the subject. Following is a sampling of some of the responses that the negotiator made to the subject:

- Will you come out? If I give you my word? Will you come out of the truck?
- I want you to be there for them.
- Show Betty that you are sincere and want to make things better.
- We'll work through it together and we'll get Betty involved. It will be better for you and your children.
- Give me an opportunity to help you.
- I know a lot about you because I spoke with Betty. (Negotiator related what he knew.)
- I'm here because I don't want to see you get hurt.
- Will you promise me you will come out? (After he asked to hear her voice on the police radio.)
- I'm not here to tell you what you want to hear. I'm here to help you.

- I can't help you until I know that I am safe and that you are safe.
- I want to help you.
- Give her another opportunity.
- I'm trying to give you some options. We can work together to try to work this out.
- Once I know you are safe, we can begin working out everything else.
- I told you she cares about you. Give her the opportunity to show you.
- As long as you keep trying, there is always the possibility that things can work out.
- I want to see you work out things with Betty and things get better.
- Will you give me the opportunity to help you?
- I'm only here to help you. I'm concerned about you and want to be sure you are okay.
- I'll do everything I can to get you and Betty to work things out. Give me the opportunity.
- It's getting late, kids are tired, you're tired, I'm tired.
- If you're serious about making your marriage work, that is what you need to do (come out).
- Are you willing to work with me on that? If I give you my word?
- I can't do that right now. They won't let me.
- The problem is that you can't make things work from inside that truck.
- You've had problems in the past and you've always managed to work them out.
- Will you come out for me?
- Let's start to work this out.
- I can't hear you, Steven.
- I want to help you, but I can only do it when I know you are safe.
- This is what I want you to do: throw out the gun and come out.
- I know you want to do the right thing and that's the right thing to do (throw gun out and come out).
- I give you my word. I will let you hear her voice if you come out.
- You're doing the right thing by wanting to talk to someone and work things out.

Steven came out at 0609.

Why Did This Work?

I think we know that it did *not* work

1. because all went perfectly;
2. because the methods that were used were somehow scientific;
3. because of "magic"; or
4. because of superhuman skills.

All may have worked out the way that it did due to luck. My guess is, however, that luck combined with the following actually allowed success to be achieved:

- Perseverance
- Procedures
- Voice quality
- Identifying with a human need
- Reading the signs
- Team involvement
- Time, after starting to intervene
- Increasing pressure
- Calculating responses
- Winning attitude
- Going for a "win-win"
- Intelligence utilization
- Letting the victim know that his feelings were heard and understood
- Noting his investment in other parts of his life (e.g., family, kitten, mission)
- Knowledge of his psychological status
- Letting him know that he was not alone
- Persistence in not leaving until the victim was safe
- Care for the victim after he came out
- Making promises that could be kept
- Sowing seeds of doubt
- Accepting his concessions
- Taking his problems seriously
- Taking our problems and personal needs seriously
- Caring for each member of our team
- Inner confidence that we could make it happen

- Good leadership
- Team-team cooperation
- Determination
- Wearing down the victim

And maybe a little more luck. Remember that good luck is usually the result of careful planning.

Chapter 9

Attending to Special Issues

Special issues present themselves before, during, and even after a hostage or crisis situation. The following are provided to assist in understanding and resolving these issues. Most are self-explanatory or have individual explanations provided.

CONSIDER RISK FACTORS

First developed by the Federal Bureau of Investigation, a list of high-risk factors in a hostage or barricade situation has been identified to assist negotiators. These factors provide indicators suggesting a substantial risk of violence in the particular situation at hand. Use them with care. Note that the cumulative value of the factors may indicate even greater risk. If any of the factors are identified, SWAT and command should be notified of the risk and of the potential need for tactical intervention in order to resolve the situation. Negotiations should continue, if possible. At the point at which negotiations are no longer possible, SWAT and command should again be notified. A tactical resolution should be considered and planned. These factors can be evaluated along with the specific items identified on the violence risk analysis worksheet (see pages 97-99). Although not an exhaustive list, some of the factors include the following:

1. The actions of the subject in this particular hostage or barricaded scene would lead one to conclude that he or she wanted to get the police involved with him or her at this time. The actions of the subject were purposeful in this regard.
2. The person being detained by the subject was specifically selected rather than being held as a matter of random circum-

stance. The subject may have had, or could be currently having, some sort of involvement with the selectee.

3. The police have been called to deal with this subject before. The situation may have been similar to the current one, but also may have involved personal violence, restraining orders, the court system in this regard, or other similar problems.

4. Detention of another person without substantive demands, as would be found in a true hostage situation.

5. Threats against the person being detained that seem to be personal rather than general in nature. A hostage taker, for instance, may make threats to hurt or kill someone for not doing as he or she asks during the siege. This individual seems to personalize the threats, and it may seem that they stem from something ongoing between the two individuals.

6. This actor has done this type of thing before.

7. When you evaluate the stress level present in the subject's life, either currently or in the recent past, it is high and extremely significant to the person. The actor may be in crisis or have experienced singular or multiple crisis situations in his or her life that are not resolved or that they believe cannot be resolved. Remember, crisis is in the eye of the beholder. If the subject thinks that he or she is experiencing a crisis, for the subject, he or she is in crisis. Try to understand the subject within this framework in order to be successful.

8. The background and rearing of the subject in this situation believes that he or she cannot back down without being personally degraded as a person. For instance, the subject's reluctance to surrender seems to be tied more to what others will think than to the practicality of peacefully resolving the situation and getting on with life. There is no "honorable" way out, would be another example. Negotiations may seem to be productive with this person, and then turn sour for seemingly no other explainable reason.

9. As part of the crisis, or impending crisis, in the subject's life, he or she feels that there is no one to whom he or she can turn for nurture and/or support. The subject feels alone and isolated without the social support systems that most of us have and can turn to in times of severe stress and crisis. This should not be interpreted to mean that no such systems exist; only

that the subject believes that they are nonexistent or non-available to him or her.

10. The subject tells you that he or she is going to commit suicide. Take this seriously regardless of the context. People who talk about suicide do take their own lives. As you may see, this statement of intent may be tied to some of the other factors mentioned. Even if the subject recants the threat, continue to monitor for the possibility of suicide, and actively make plans to counter such an attempt and/or to suggest a rescue of the subject.

11. The subject's verbalizations seem to change direction and sound more and more like a final spiritual confession. This may happen in combination with a suicidal statement or seem to stand alone. Remember that the direction in which they are headed is the same. The subject may ask you to tell his or her family certain things, or to have someone retrieve certain documents for him or her, etc. The subject may ask for extended time off of the phone in order to "take care of some things" or to "make some decisions." Listen carefully for this change of emphasis. From a negotiating standpoint, you may want to interrupt this line of verbalization rather than allow it to continue. If the subject cannot complete the confession, he or she may not feel that he or she can kill himself or herself. If you suspect suicide, regardless of the verbalizations to the contrary, you may want to try to keep the subject on the phone rather than allowing him or her to disconnect and remain alone.

UTILIZE THE VIOLENCE RISK ANALYSIS WORKSHEET

The violence risk analysis worksheet is derived from current information regarding those factors that predispose and may predict likelihood of violence. These violence risk analysis items have been adapted, in part, from the high-risk factors developed for negotiators by the FBI. It should be regarded as a guideline only. Obviously, the more factors that are present, the greater the possibility of violence. The greater the number of more serious factors that are present, the even greater risk of violence that exists. More factors may equal greater risk. More serious factors present may equal an even greater risk. Use this worksheet with care.

_____ 1. The situation experienced by the actor is the result of a family dispute or divorce, especially if children are involved.

_____ 2. History of causing deliberate encounters with the police or confrontations with other authorities relative to a personal case before the court or in regard to orders of the court.

_____ 3. Current or historical use of minor children as a tool, pawn, or weapon against the other spouse in a family dispute.

_____ 4. Historical problems, singular or serial, severe enough to warrant police intervention.

_____ 5. The conflict experienced involves allegations of child abuse or spousal abuse.

_____ 6. Where there are allegations of abuse, a complaint has been filed by either or both parties which has been, or is about to be, presented in court.

_____ 7. Direct threats from one party against another or by third parties against either or both parties.

_____ 8. Expressed feelings of powerlessness or helplessness to affect the outcome of one's own dispute with another.

_____ 9. Outbursts which reflect feelings that judicial authorities or others involved with the actor are part of a conspiracy to thwart the actor's efforts.

_____10. History of difficult court appearances or ineffective legal battles.

_____11. Unusual interest in, or expenditures of limited personal resources for, reforming an inadequate, unfair, or unjust judicial, social, professional or employment system. Such interests or expenditures seem disproportionate to other activities in the actor's life.

_____12. History of or recent multiple life stressors either directly related or unrelated to the current conflict experienced by the actor.

_____13. High levels of personal dissatisfaction with one's life.

_____14. Cultural background of the actor that emphasizes a major importance of "loss of face," or of male dominance in relationships.

___15. Perceived or actual lack of personal support systems. May be seen as a loner or as interested in nonhuman interactions.

___16. Verbalizations concerning homicide or suicide.

___17. Verbalizations concerning the taking and holding of hostages, especially family members.

___18. Verbalizations concerning "setting affairs in order," or which may sound similar to the making of a "verbal will."

___19. History of impulsive acts.

___20. A "gut feeling" by those observing the actor that something is about to happen of a violent nature.

___21. Recent purchase of a weapon and ammunition absent a historical interest in such items.

___22. History of high interest in weapons coupled with substantial recent purchases of weapons or ammunition.

___23. History of perceived or actual multiple personal losses.

___24. History of multiple life changes within a relatively short time period.

___25. A diagnosed psychiatric disorder.

___26. Inappropriately subdued affect, or behavior that is an inconsistent reaction to the actual issues at hand.

___27. History of previous violent acts.

___28. History, as a child, of violent acts with animals.

___29. A developmental history that indicates a lack of early, constant, and nurturing attachments.

___30. Subject grew up within an impulsive family structure or in an overly controlled family.

___31. Violence in subject's family of orientation seen as a mode of communication.

___32. Peer group of the subject endorses violence.

___33. History of, or current, job instability.

___34. Medical history of central nervous system (CNS) trauma or current subjective CNS symptoms such as complaints of dizziness, blackouts, amnesia, memory loss, headaches, nausea, episodic rage, or sense of confusion with remorse.

___35. Objective CNS signs.

REVIEW RED FLAG INDICATORS
AND PAY ATTENTION TO THEM

Red flags are indicators that an actor may be mentally ill, potentially violent, or reacting to misuse of substances. These indicators may be provided by the actor, the actor's parents, children, or other friends or acquaintances of the family. Such indicators may be clues to the mental status of the subject but should not be regarded as absolute proof. Absent these indicators, the actor may still be mentally ill and/or become violent with negotiators/interveners. If the negotiator has any reason, internal or external, to believe that the actor is mentally ill or that the actor may become violent, care should be taken when approaching the subject in a face-to-face situation. In addition, any of these phrases should be investigated further by the negotiator to clarify their meaning and the possible risks.

"What do you mean by that?"
"How so?"
"Could you tell me more about that?"
"What makes you say that?"
"What does she do that makes you say that?"
"What exactly did he say to you?"
"Could you explain your comments to me?"

Often, the answers to these questions will be clarifying.

Caution: Some of the following are phrases that the negotiator/ intervener should not use in referring to any person. They are phrases or comments that the negotiator may hear from others that may provide clues to the mental status of the actor. They are provided for this purpose only.

"He seems angry."
"She is always very angry."
"Something is wrong with him."
"I don't know what is the matter with that person."
"He seems strange."
"He just walks around all day doing nothing."
"He always argues with the children in the neighborhood."
"He just came up and hit him for no reason."
"She is always yelling and screaming at anyone who comes by."

"He's crazy."

"She is just weird."

"He mumbles to himself."

"She accuses me of being out to get her."

"She has tinfoil over all of her windows."

"She threatened to kill me if I come over to her house."

"I don't understand what is going on with him."

"He just doesn't seem right."

"He is a real oddball."

"Sometimes, I can't understand her."

"He will talk to me and I can't make out what he means."

"He told me that aliens were going to come and get him."

"He says that nobody believes him."

"My children are afraid of her."

"I am afraid of him."

"She dresses funny."

"He sometimes walks around the street with some of his clothes off."

"Someone said that he had been in a mental hospital."

"He goes off for no reason."

"She never comes out of her house."

"She has got a twenty-foot cross nailed to the roof of her house."

"I don't know what to make of him."

"The kids think that he's strange."

"Man, he's off."

"You're going to need some help."

"I don't know about him."

"She walks around doing things that make no sense."

"He's always looking behind him like someone is after him."

"He's a brick short of a load."

"When I try to talk to him, he just jumps from one subject to another."

"I'm not sure that he is really doing very well."

"She needs help."

"He's nice enough, but sometimes he goes over the edge."

"When I am around him, I feel all creepy."

"The kids always make fun of her."

"He wears these strange clothes."

"I think he's off his medication/not taking his medicine."

"I think that he has been in and out of hospitals."
"She has a lot of pill bottles in her house."
"He's loony."
"He's at it again."
"She's really from outer space."
"Sometimes he goes off on me."
"He's really off his rocker."

KNOW WHEN TO TERMINATE UTILITIES

Knowing when to terminate the utilities that operate within a hostage or barricade stronghold requires special attention. At one time in the history of our discipline it was accepted procedure to automatically terminate all utilities almost immediately, but this particular decision requires revisiting. In light of more current thinking, the following guidelines are suggested:

1. Avoid terminating utilities after arriving on the scene until a thorough evaluation of the situation has been made by SWAT, command, and negotiators.
2. Immediate termination of utilities should be done only if special circumstances exist as determined by those evaluating the incident.
3. Before deciding to terminate any utility, ask, "Why should these be terminated at this particular time?"
4. Ask, "What has changed in the immediate past that would necessitate termination?"
5. Ask, "What advantage will be gained by shutting off utilities?"
6. Consider advantages that may accrue to the hostage taker if some or all utilities are terminated.
7. Are there medical or psychological concerns that may be enhanced or degraded? Hostages? Hostage taker? Crisis victim? Suicidal subject?
8. Be aware of weather conditions when making a decision about utilities. For example, if it is cold outside, will it do

much good to cut off the air-conditioning? Cutting the heat may be more effective.

9. Once interrupted, can the utility or utilities be reestablished, if necessary?

10. What authority, if any, is needed before utilities can be terminated?

11. Are personnel from the various utilities available to disconnect them? Will you need to improvise and do it yourself? Is this a job for SWAT?

12. If you are trying to capture a phone line, do you know who to speak to at the telephone company? In the middle of the night? It is usually a good idea to make these arrangements prior to the occurrence of an incident. Phone companies have security procedures that must be followed in order to interrupt and divert service. Contacting the operator in the middle of the night, without prior planning, may not get the needed results.

13. Are there financial costs involved in shutting down a utility? For example, shutting off electricity to a convenience store may turn off refrigerators containing perishables.

14. Remember that the termination of a utility or all utilities will have some effect on someone. The more that you can anticipate in this regard, the more prepared and effective you will be.

15. Utilities termination should benefit the authorities, not the subject. This is true unless you want the termination to benefit the subject. You should be in a position to control this.

16. If reinstating utilities can be used as a bargaining tool, so much the better.

17. If you agree to turn something on again, be sure that you can do it. Your credibility is at risk.

18. Always have a reason for what you do, or do not do. Never do something just to see what happens.

19. Discuss options with your team members on the scene. Get additional information as needed.

20. Be careful about utilities. They can help you or hurt you. Nothing, in this regard, should be automatic. Of course, there may be individual exceptions for a team to consider.

KNOW HOW TO WIN AND LOSE AS A TEAM

As negotiators, we expect to win. We are taught that our skills and techniques will achieve success nearly all of the time. Generally, we are not disappointed. We spend a lot of time learning what to do; we do it; we win. But, not always. If you work in this field long enough, you may well be involved in a situation that does not turn out as you would hope. What happens after that could be the real measure of a negotiations team. It is relatively easy to accept a successful resolution. It is not so easy to deal with a loss. How you do it could affect a team's ability to function effectively in the future. How your department reacts is but another variable. The following are ten steps designed to help you better handle this inevitable eventuality.

Step one: Acknowledge the problem—ownership of the victim.

Step two: Recognize that the feelings felt by the negotiator and the negotiating team, regarding the loss of life, are to be expected and are normal.

Step three: Try not to see a tactical resolution as a negotiations failure.

Step four: Be supportive of the feelings of others without the need to "second-guess."

Step five: Do what you can to ensure the continued support of the department, regardless of outcome.

Step six: If professional help is needed, seek it early to maximize its benefits. Encourage others to do the same.

Step seven: Talk about what you feel with someone you trust (e.g., other negotiators, a family member, or close friend).

Step eight: Remember that although feelings cannot be changed voluntarily, behaviors can. What you do may eventually have some effect on what you feel.

Step nine: Do not take credit for the "saves," and you need not take responsibility for the losses.

Step ten: Work as a team. Win as a team. Lose as a team. Support one another as a team.

Being taken hostage under any circumstance is a difficult situation to be in regardless of who you are or what you do. Being taken hostage if you are a law enforcement officer creates additional problems and pressures. This is true both for the hostage taker and for the peace officer. Also, it may create a stressful situation for the other, non-law enforcement hostages who may expect you to "do something." For these reasons, the following guidelines are provided. Please take them seriously. Remember that if you are going to try to escape your captors, the best time to do it will be immediately after being captured. You will be in the best physical and mental condition at that time for resisting. If you decide not to resist, then it becomes important that you do what is necessary to prevent harm to the other hostage or to yourself. The better you understand the guidelines, hopefully, the better you will be able to manage your situation until you are rescued.

KNOW HOW TO SURVIVE
IF YOU ARE TAKEN HOSTAGE

- Don't try to be a hero. Accept your situation, and be prepared to wait.
- Follow instructions. Remember that the first fifteen to forty-five minutes are the most dangerous.
- Do not speak unless spoken to, and then only when necessary.
- Try to rest and maintain your strength.
- Don't make suggestions to the hostage taker.
- Do not try to escape unless you are absolutely sure that you will be successful.
- If you need medical attention or medication, inform your captors.
- Be observant. You may be released, or escape, and your information may be helpful.
- Be prepared to answer the police/negotiator on the phone. Only give "yes" or "no" answers.
- Don't become argumentative.
- Treat your captors like "royalty."
- Be patient.
- During a rescue attempt, lie low. When the police come in, make no sudden moves.
- Keep other captives calm. Reassure them that help is coming.
- Remember, because you are a hostage, you will be regarded as such by the police. (Bolz, 1979, p. 313. Used with permission.)

CONSIDER THE ROLE OF TACTICAL EMERGENCY MEDICAL SUPPORT FOR NEGOTIATORS

The use of tactical medics by members of hostage and crisis negotiations teams has not been examined in the literature or in the field. Usually, negotiations teams are deployed within the confines of the established inner perimeter along with the tactical team and tactical medics. Although the likelihood of injuries or performance-degrading medical problems for negotiators is less than that expected for SWAT team members, they may occur and need attention. In addition, tactical medical personnel can play other roles that are specific to the needs of police negotiators.

Introduction

Since the early 1990s, the role of tactical emergency medical support for law enforcement has been scrutinized and debated. Based in part on the military field medical model, the need for such support to special weapons and tactics teams has taken on considerable importance in the police service. Injuries occur during deployment and during training. Access to immediate medical and dental care can often reduce the consequences of the injuries and provide frontline life saving measures when necessary. Medical personnel also help to fill the role of preventative medicine officer and safety officer, ensuring that the team leader is aware of potentially performance-degrading environmental conditions or situations. As is the case with the military, unit morale is often affected in a positive way because of the presence of unit level medical personnel.

History

Law enforcement is a dangerous occupation. According to the U.S. Department of Justice (2003), FBI, Uniform Crime Report, every year at least fifty-two police officers are feloniously killed and more than 26,000 are injured as a result of assaults occurring in the line of duty. Data from the Casualty Care Research Center at the Uniformed Services University of the Health Sciences suggest that, "SWAT team members are at high risk for injury, sustaining a casualty rate of approximately 8.9 per 1000 for tactical officers in training missions" (CONTOMS, 1993, p. 2).

The Counter Narcotics Tactical Operations Medical Support Program, otherwise known as CONTOMS, is a cooperative effort between the Department of Defense, Uniformed Services University, the Department of the Interior, the United States Park Police Special Forces Branch, and the Henry M. Jackson Foundation for the Advancement of Military Medicine. This program was begun in 1990 to meet the special needs of tactical law enforcement for frontline medical support above and beyond that which is usually provided at the scene of police tactical incidents. The basic training is for trained EMTs or higher, and consists of fifty-eight hours of training to qualify as a tactical emergency medical technician.

TEMS and the Hostage and Crisis Negotiator

Medical support for negotiators injured during actual operations and while in training is of obvious importance. What may not be so obvious are the ways in which tactical medics can support the primary activities of police negotiators. The following is a true story that illustrates the value to negotiators of the tactical medic.

Case Study

As usual, it was the middle of the night and it was unseasonably cold. The barricaded subject told the first negotiator who contacted him that he had shot himself in the shoulder with a rifle. In fact, a noise, thought to be a gunshot, was heard by the deployed SWAT team. As negotiations got under way, the subject complained of his wound and was also observed at an apartment window with a towel over the reported site of his wound. The negotiations team sergeant requested that a tactical medic come to the negotiations command post to listen to the ongoing negotiations with the subject. Tactical medics have specialized training in what is called, "medicine across the barricade" and remote medical assessments. Defined, medicine across the barricade refers to the special skills of the tactical medic that allow a medical, and sometimes a psychological, assessment and treatment to be done using information about the subject provided telephonically by a third person collocated with the barricaded person and hostages or by direct conversation. Such information may also be obtained by direct remote observations of the victim made by the tactical medic from a secure distant position in the field. Therefore the medic might be able to do a rapid assessment and to provide additional intelligence information and confirmations to the negotiations team.

Based on the medical assessment done by the medic in our situation, it was determined that the subject was not injured at all. Later, on surrender, this proved to be exactly the case. Knowing the medical status of the subject early in the negotiations process enabled negotiators to concentrate on the more pressing psychological aspects of their job. Without such information, the approach to the subject might have been changed inappropriately and thus have adversely affected the outcome.

In addition, the subject told the negotiator that he was taking certain medications. Once this was discovered, the tactical EMT on-scene with the team was able to provide information concerning the use and actions of the reported medications. Usual dosages and side effects were valuable pieces of intelligence that would help round out the picture of the person to whom the negotiator was talking.

As the night wore on, some concerns were expressed for negotiators, who, for various reasons, had been exposed to the cold weather. Medics available to the team were able to offer preventative assistance and guidance in this regard.

The negotiations continued for about six hours and although done well, seemed to be constantly foiled by the subject's fear that, upon surrender, he would be taken for an involuntary mental health commitment and psychological evaluation. Later, we found out that his concerns were based on a similar previous encounter. He countered the negotiator's appeal for surrender with his concern about being taken to the hospital and assured all concerned that nothing was wrong with him. Further, he said that if he did not have to go to the hospital, he would surrender peacefully.

The police psychologist assigned to the negotiations team, who is also CONTOMS trained, suggested that because of what we knew about him both physically and psychologically, that the negotiator suggest to the subject that it might be possible to bring a psychologist to the scene to evaluate him immediately upon his surrender and thereby to determine the actual need for an involuntary mental commitment. Since he believed that there was nothing wrong with him, such an evaluation might yield negative results. If so, he could then return to his apartment. He agreed and the surrender was planned and executed. Both negotiator and police psychologist met with the subject outside his apartment after his uneventful surrender to SWAT officers. A medical and psychological assessment was done as promised. Based on the evaluations, the subject agreed to the need for additional mental health evaluation and was transported. The combined efforts of the negotiator, negotiations team, tactical medic, tactical medical and psychologically trained police psychologist, and the SWAT team brought this situation to a successful conclusion. The importance of the tactical medic in this instance should be clear. Above and beyond providing medical care, support of the ongoing negotiations proved invaluable.

Multiple Roles

The roles of the tactical medic when supporting a hostage and crisis negotiations team, and acting as a resource to it, might be, but are not limited to, the following:

1. Medicine across the barricade
2. Assessment of barricaded subject and hostage taker during negotiations
3. Information on medications used by the subject
4. Assessment of subject's postsurrender
5. Preventative medicine for negotiators
6. Consultation concerning intelligence information gathered on the subject
7. Medical care to negotiators
8. Consultation on medical options for the subject both during and after the incident
9. Remote assessments of the subject when visual contact is possible
10. Threat assessments related to location of the negotiations command post and deployment of negotiations equipment

Implications

The use of tactical medics is growing throughout the country. This is true, in large part, because of the work of the Casualty Care Research Center in Bethesda, Maryland. Support of SWAT teams in the field and during training scenarios is increasing as police, fire department, and emergency services personnel come to understand what the military has always known: quality, precision medical care in the front lines saves lives, raises morale, and requires specialized training.

Similar support for teams deployed with SWAT teams, such as hostage and crisis negotiations teams, has not been explored or anticipated. The use of the tactical medic with such teams goes beyond the delivery of medical services in the more traditional sense. As outlined, the role of the tactical medic can be expanded to provide invaluable information both to the primary negotiator and to the intelligence section of a negotiations team. Such information may be the difference between successful and nonsuccessful resolution of a hostage or barricaded incident.

Chapter 10

Specific Issues Relating to Suicide

REVIEW THE PROCEDURES FOR RESPONDING TO A SUICIDAL SUBJECT

1. Act early. If you suspect suicide, take action now! Don't wait until it's too late. Make contact early. Do not leave the sufferer alone. Time will not work here for the negotiator.
2. Speak of suicide openly. If you can talk openly about it, maybe it will be easier for the sufferer to speak of it. Using the word *suicide* will not make the person suicidal. Tell the sufferer, "I don't want you to die." Listen carefully to what is said. Reassure and remain calm. The sufferer may think that you are there to arrest him or her. He or she may also challenge your sincerity. Let the sufferer talk and let him or her know that you are trying to understand his or her hurt.
3. Never say, "You don't really want to do that." The sufferer really does want to do it.
4. Never ask, "Why do you want to do that?" The sufferer probably does not know "why," and the question will increase his or her defensiveness. Ask present-oriented questions if you need information: "What happened?"; "How do you feel?"; "What's going on?"; "Would you like to talk about it?"
5. Remember that a suicidal person will have trouble focusing on the future and that, "Things will get better." Keep your focus on the present and what can be done to assist the sufferer now.
6. Never challenge the sufferer to "Go ahead and do it." You may be giving him or her permission to do the act that you will regret for the rest of your life. If weapons are present, try to remove them, or to convince the subject that putting down the weapon will make things safer for you and the subject. Do not

focus too much on the weapon. You can successfully intervene in this situation even if a weapon is present. Regardless, always protect yourself when weapons, or other potential dangers, are present.

7. Be careful of whom you call to talk, or whom you allow to talk, with the victim. They may be part of the problem (e.g., family members, minister, doctor). The best person to handle a suicidal individual is a trained police negotiator.

8. Remember that suicide has nothing to do with death. Suicide has to do with conflict in a person's life between the sufferer and at least one other person or institution, either present or absent, in his or her life at the moment. Death may be only the unfortunate by-product of the suicidal gesture.

9. If you believe that the person is suicidal, do not leave him or her alone. If physically with the person, stay with him or her or get someone else to stay if you have to leave. If on the phone, stay on the phone with the person to the degree that you can. If you must get off the phone, or if the subject gets off the phone, make contact again without unnecessary delay.

10. Rule of thumb: Check out the "specificity of the suicidal plan," and the "lethality of the suicidal means." The more specific the plan and the more lethal the means, the greater the risk of suicide. Ask the sufferer what he or she intends to do and how. There may come a time during a suicide intervention when you believe that the subject is about to act on his or her suicide plan. At such a time, a tactical or combined tactical and negotiation resolution may be necessary. Always have such a plan in place for such an eventuality.

KNOW HOW TO USE THE LETHALITY SCALE

The rule of thumb previously referred to can be of help in a field situation when a quick assessment of suicidality is needed. However, the lethality scale can provide additional and considerably more detailed information for making this evaluation. It takes time to utilize the scale correctly. It can also be utilized throughout the incident as more information about the subject or victims becomes available. As the accuracy of the information utilized increases, the usefulness of the scale also increases. See Box 10.1 for a sample of the scale.

BOX 10.1.
The Lethality Scale of the American Academy of Crisis Interveners

	O Points	1 Point	2 Points	3 Points	4 Points	Total
Age, male	0-12 yrs.		13-44 yrs.	45-64 yrs.	65 and up	
Age, female	0-12 yrs.	13-44 yrs.	45 and up			
Personal resources available	Good	Fair		Poor		
Current stress	Low		Medium		High	
Marital status	Married, children	Married, no children		Widowed or single	Divorced	
Current psychological functioning	Stable		Unstable			
Other problems or symptoms	Absent		Present			
Communication channels	Open		Blocked			
Physical condition	Good	Fair			Poor	
Suicide by close family member	No		Yes			
Depressed or agitated currently	No				Yes	
Prior suicidal behavior by subject	No		Yes			

(continued)

(continued)

	O Points	1 Point	2 Points	3 Points	4 Points	Total
Reactions by significant others to the needs of the subject	Helpful			Not helpful		
Current financial stress	Absent		Present			
Suicidal plan of the subject	Has none	Plan with few details	Subject has selected the means for suicide		Subject has a highly specific plan for suicide	
Occupation of subject	Non-helping profession or other occupation	MD, dentist, attorney, or helping professional	Psychiatrist, police officer, or unemployed			
Residence	Rural	Suburban	Urban			
Living arrangements	Lives with others				Lives alone	
Time of the year this incident is occurring		Spring				
Day of the week this incident is occurring		Sunday or Wednesday	Monday			
Recent occurrence of serious arguments with spouse or significant other	No	Yes				

(continued)

(continued)

Recently, the subject's significant other was:	The focus of a dis- appoint- ment	Lost to the sub- ject in some sig- nificant way		
				Total Points

Name of subject:
Date and time scale completed:
Name of negotiator completing this scale:
Comments and action notes:

Criteria

Minimal risk (0-15 points)   _____
Low risk (16-30 points)   _____
Medium risk (31-46 points)   _____
High risk (47-60 points)   _____

Directions for Use: Circle response in appropriate row and column. Place points from top of column in the far right column. Sum all scores under total points and match with total criteria. Scale can be run multiple times on same subject as more information becomes available.

(*Source:* Dr. Edward S. Rosenbluh. Reprinted with permission.)

RECOGNIZE A "SUICIDE BY COP": VICTIM-PRECIPITATED SUICIDE

This is a very dangerous situation in which the suicidal person may use the police to accomplish the suicidal act. You may be talking to a potential "suicide by cop" person if he or she

- demands to be killed by you or by your department;
- sets deadlines for his or her own death;
- requests additional weapons;
- has just killed a "significant other" in his or her life (e.g., spouse, parent, or a young child);
- provides you with a "verbal will"; and/or
- has an elaborate plan for his or her death.

This person represents a significant threat to hostages, himself or herself, and negotiators and other law enforcement officers. This individual may take an officer's life in order to cause a deadly response by SWAT officers. He or she may kill a negotiator who has elected to go face to face.

CONFRONTING ADOLESCENT SUICIDE

The teenage years are a period of turmoil as many changes are taking place both emotionally and physically and new social roles are being learned. Sometimes solutions to problems are not readily available to the teen and the result can be loneliness. The more that negotiators understand about the unique nature of teen suicidal actors, the better prepared they will be to intervene effectively.

People speculate about how their lives will be and what they should do to make it so. With teens, it can be particularly difficult to understand all that is going on around them. Family problems, divorce, embarrassment, and even poor grades in school can exacerbate a sense of great concern about one's life and the reasons to continue or to end it. Teens may have some difficulty recognizing the bigger picture that just as things change, so do feelings and inner turmoil. It may become too much to handle for the young mind and depression can result. Such depression increases the risk of suicidal behavior. There may be a need for support during these times and such support might come from a parent, a good friend, or a mental health professional. However, recognition of the problem by those closest to the teen is the first step in the process toward better mental help at these times. Denial will not make the problem go away. Undoubtedly, it will make the problem worse as the loneliness and the feelings of not being understood increase. To the contrary, with effective help, most can recover from the depression fairly quickly.

What to Look For

Mood swings are normal. Everyone feels sad at times. Feeling sad is not our focus here. A depressed mood that continues for two weeks or more could be a significant sign that deserves attention. Listen to what teens say and what they do. Help could be needed if you hear:

"I am sleeping much later than I used to," "I'm not sleeping well and I wake up early in the morning," or "I am beginning to take a lot of naps." Changes in appetite and unplanned weight gain or loss are additional clues. Remember that you do not have to be a psychologist to pay attention to the signs of suicide in teenagers or to take appropriate action when needed.

Listen for the following verbal cues:

"I feel restless."
"I have withdrawn from friends and family."
"I can't concentrate very well."
"I've lost interest or pleasure in my usual activities."
"I feel guilty" or "I feel hopeless and helpless."
"I used to be outgoing; now I seem to be withdrawing."
"I have sudden mood changes."
"I really feel that life is not worth living anymore."

More Clues

- Young people who have attempted suicide in the past are at greater risk.
- Those who talk about suicide may actually do it. It is a myth to think otherwise.
- Feelings of loneliness, hopelessness, and rejection are characteristics of those teens who may consider killing themselves.
- Teens who abuse alcohol or drugs are more likely to consider, attempt, or succeed at suicide than are nonabusers.
- Teens who may be planning to kill themselves may give away personal possessions, discard things that are usually meaningful to them, or begin cleaning their own room.
- The teen may suddenly become cheerful, or even appear upbeat, after a bout with depression. The sudden change may foretell that he or she has made the decision to end his or her own life. Do not put off getting help in these circumstances.
- Remember that one of the most dangerous times occurs when severe loss of any kind has been experienced or personal humiliation has been felt.

Some Findings

1. Those who talk of helplessness and hopelessness may be at greater risk.
2. Talking about suicide will not prevent it from happening as some believe.
3. Depression and the ultimate risk of suicide may have biological as well as psychological causes.
4. A family history of suicide may be a significant risk factor in predicting suicidal behavior in teens.
5. The suicide rate for teens is about the same as the national average. Although not as high as the media would have us believe, suicide among teenagers is a serious health problem.
6. Males seem to commit suicide more than do females. Females attempt suicide more often, however.

Negotiation Guidelines

The American Psychiatric Association and the American Psychological Association provide much insight into teen suicide and suicide intervention. Many times persons who are depressed, or depressed and suicidal, will find it hard to talk to anyone about what they feel. Feelings of worthlessness and hopelessness may contribute to this unwillingness to reach out to others. They may even deny their own emotions or think that talking to someone will only burden the listener. Remember, they may truly believe that no one cares anyway. Some may feel that they will be made fun of.

Although much of the reluctance to reach out and express themselves may be justified by previous encounters, such can make the problems worse. Many who contemplate suicide will leave some clues. In many cases the teen who is suicidal has spoken with, or at least tried to speak with, someone about what he or she is experiencing. If the teen alludes to the subject of suicide or brings it up directly, take it seriously and take some time to talk about it. The difference that this small act of talking and listening can make could be inestimable.

Reassure the troubled teen that he or she has those around him or her who are ready and willing to help. Do not be afraid to listen to the teen and to try to understand his or her dilemma of wanting to live on the one hand and die on the other. It is part of his or her experience.

Sometimes it is hard to let someone else know that there is a need to talk about something as serious as our emotions.

There is a tendency when talking with people who are suicidal to preach or to lecture to them about why they should not kill themselves. Further, it will not be very helpful to point out to teens all of the reasons that they should stay alive or the things for which they have to live. Instead, listen and reassure. I repeat for emphasis, *listen and reassure!* Depression and suicidal tendencies can be treated successfully. Tell them that also, but only after you have listened a lot and reassured as needed.

Chapter 11

Developing Negotiator Survival Skills

USE SELF-RELAXATION SKILLS

The consequences of high levels of job stress, personal frustration, and inadequate coping skills may result in major problems for negotiators and negotiation teams. Stress is not a mental illness. Stress is part of everyday living and potentially each of us is vulnerable to the disease of too much stress and too little coping ability.

The following five steps can be used almost anywhere and at any time to help minimize stress. They were adapted from some of the work done in this field by Dr. Edward S. Rosenbluh. During this total relaxation, your mind remains alert. As long as you do not do the steps for longer than twenty minutes, you are not likely to fall asleep. When you are finished, you will feel relaxed and fresh. Experienced relaxers even talk of a "natural high" produced without drugs.

When time or circumstances do not permit following the whole program, you may do parts of it. It can be done with your eyes open or closed. It can be done for short periods of time. It can even be done in a meeting, as a passenger in a vehicle, during breaks or downtime, and during other appropriate or private times. You will feel more refreshed and alert even after a short session than if you had remained tense the entire time.

> *Step one:* Sit or lie in a comfortable position. Allow the weight of all parts of your body to be supported. Lean your head forward if sitting, or back if lying down.
> *Step two:* Close your eyes and relax all parts of your body. Feel your feet getting heavy and relaxed, then your ankles, knees, hips, midsection, hands, arms, shoulders, neck, jaw, eyes, forehead, and even your tongue. Feel each part of your body,

in succession, starting with your feet, become heavy, relaxed, and comfortable.

Step three: Begin to concentrate on your breathing. Observe it with your mind as it slowly goes in and out. During each exhale, say the word "one" to yourself (e.g., inhale, exhale, "one," inhale, exhale, "one," etc.).

Step four: The word "one" will help keep meaningful thoughts from your mind. Do not worry if fleeting thoughts come in and out of focus. Concentrate on breathing and on "one."

Step five: Continue for twenty minutes. Do this once in the morning and once in the evening, as needed and as possible. Do these steps when you feel tense. You may check the clock periodically. Because of digestion, which might interfere, it would probably be best to avoid total relaxation for about two hours after eating. If you feel your hands getting warmer, this is okay. Such sensations often accompany total relaxation. Sometimes, it even helps to think about your hands and arms getting warmer after step two.

UNDERSTAND THE SIGNS OF JOB STRESS AND BURNOUT

The following signs and symptoms of job stress and burnout are provided to help team members recognize and solve stress-related difficulties early. Teams that are overstressed will not react effectively in the field when the external stress of the event is also present.

1. High resistance to going to work everyday
2. Pervasive sense of failure
3. Anger and resentment
4. Feelings of guilt and blaming of others or self
5. Discouragement and indifference
6. Negativism
7. Isolation and withdrawal
8. Feeling tired and exhausted all day
9. Frequent clock-watching
10. Unusually great fatigue after work
11. Loss of positive feeling toward others, particularly team members

12. Postponing social contacts, phone calls, etc.
13. Inability to concentrate on or to listen to information
14. Feelings of being immobilized
15. Cynicism toward team members and the team process
16. Sleep disorders
17. Unusual self-preoccupation
18. Use of medications to control behavior
19. Frequent colds and other illnesses
20. Frequent headaches and gastrointestinal disturbances
21. Rigidity in thinking as well as resistance to change
22. Unusual suspicion and feelings that others are acting antagonistically
23. Marital and/or family conflicts
24. Free-floating anxiety
25. A sense of "tunnel vision" when trying to solve problems or evaluate the external world
26. A sense of increasing helplessness
27. Fear that "It won't get any better"
28. Fear of loss of personal control
29. High rate of absenteeism
30. Feeling that no matter what you do to achieve goals, the attempts are always thwarted

DEVELOP PERSONAL SURVIVAL SKILLS

Surviving high-stress situations is a matter of personal responsibility. All of us are subject to the stresses and strains of the job. Some handle these well. Others do not. If we are serious about negotiator survival, so that we can continue to perform effectively on the job, the following will be observed and developed as personal survival skills. A commitment on your part is required for these skills to be effective.

1. Watch your diet. Eliminate foods high in fat, sugar, and salt, and beverages high in caffeine. Check with a physician before making any major changes to your diet.
2. Avoid alcohol and tobacco.
3. Exercise regularly. Rigorous physical activity, within your own capabilities and restrictions, can be an effective stress re-

ducer. Consult a physician before starting any exercise program.

4. Be realistic about the "givens" in your own life. What is, is.
5. Realistically assess your abilities.
6. Schedule time for fun.
7. Schedule time for dreaming.
8. Set aside time for recreation.
9. Get positive nurturing for yourself, as needed.
10. Set realistic goals.
11. Consider your choices and your responsibilities.
12. Seek help early, if you need it.

Chapter 12

Learning and Using Effective Communication Skills

ASK THE RIGHT QUESTIONS

Before a problem can be managed effectively, the negotiator must know what the problem is. Often, more than one problem is present in a given situation. When this occurs, questions can be asked to determine the priority for intervention.

1. Which of the problems presented is of immediate concern? Which has the highest priority as evaluated by the negotiator?
2. Which problem would prove most damaging if not dealt with immediately?
3. Which of the problems presented can be resolved the quickest?
4. Which problem must be dealt with before others can be handled?
5. What resources do I have at hand to handle the problems presented?
6. What are the barriers and obstacles currently present, or likely to be present, that will hinder problem solving?
7. Is there anything that must be done or changed now in order to enhance problem resolution or management? Why do I want to change these things at the current time? Why not change them? Has anything occurred to necessitate the anticipated change? If not, why change?

Although it is necessary to answer these questions, the negotiator must be able to acquire the needed information quickly and accurately. Some of the information needed will come from external sources, but the negotiator will gather much that must be known from the subject directly. This means that the negotiator must listen actively to the subject's total message and give the actor full concentration and undivided attention. Further, the negotiator must sift through the subject's words to gain information and insight into the person's problems and views of those problems.

UNDERSTAND THE MESSAGES

Every communication from the hostage taker contains three messages:

1. *Content:* This message provides information about what the sender believes, thinks, or perceives the situation to be.
2. *Feeling:* The feeling message conveys the nature and intensity of the sender's emotion about the current or related situations.
3. *Meaning:* This concerns the behavior or situation that has generated the feeling.

Usually, the person who sends the communication implies, rather than explicitly stating, the behavior or situation that creates the feelings. The negotiator must try to infer what the behavior or situation is.

UNDERSTAND THE NATURE OF DISTORTIONS

Dr. Edward S. Rosenbluh, a pioneer in the field of crisis intervention, explained that when another person communicates with you, distortions can occur in three main areas:

1. What the subject means to say
2. What the subject actually says
3. What you, as the negotiator, believe that you hear

BE EMPATHETIC

The key to effective listening is accurately hearing the feelings and meanings behind the content of any communication. This is often referred to as the skill of empathy. Empathy is the ability to enter the subject's world, and to reflect your understanding of this world, to the subject. Empathy contains two elements:

1. *Passive empathy:* This is the ability to hear the facts contained in the words and the feelings contained in the subject's body language, intensity, and tone.
2. *Active empathy:* Active empathy refers to the ability to reflect this understanding to the other person in a manner that generates warmth, trust, and a willingness to be open. This is often a difficult skill for novice negotiators and the more experienced alike. Practice, practice, practice. The tendency is to take the police approach and deal only with surface facts. An inability to get below the surface of these facts will reduce the negotiator's effectiveness of bringing the situation to a successful conclusion. Now go back and read the previous sentence again.

NEVER ASSUME

Sometimes a victim or a hostage taker will make a statement that the negotiator does not fully understand. At other times, the subject's words and nonverbal behavior may not agree. At such a point, the negotiator must focus on the misunderstanding and try to clarify the statement made prior to continuing with the intervention. Negotiators must not assume that they understand what the subject means. The negotiator must find out and know what the subject means. Conversely, two people can have very different experiences, and relate these experiences similarly. Negotiators must be sure that they know precisely what the subject is talking about. To do so, the intervener must

1. Press the subject to clarify vague or ambiguous statements
2. Be sure that the subject and the negotiator are talking about the same thing at the same time

CLARIFY STATEMENTS

Techniques for clarifying statements of the subject include the following:

1. Repeating key words
    a. Repeat key words or phrases that the subject uses.
    b. Focus on a specific word or phrase that is not clearly understood. This may cause the subject to clarify the meaning.
    c. Encourage the subject to explain in more detail.
    d. Be careful using this technique. Repeating can sound insincere.
    e. Parroting may make the subject distrustful of, or uneasy with, the negotiator.
    f. This is a useful tool when used cautiously.
2. Restatement
    a. Rephrase what the subject says as a way of encouraging him or her to clarify meaning.
    b. Restatement may cause the subject to talk more about areas of his or her life or situation that are most pressing.
    c. Encourages the subject or victim to provide more detail.
    d. The additional information gained using this technique will help the negotiator to understand what the subject is thinking and feeling.
3. The direct method
    a. This technique is very effective.
    b. The negotiator admits that he or she is confused or puzzled about the subject's statement.
    c. Ask the subject for clarification.
    d. Explain that this clarification will result in better understanding on the negotiator's part.
    e. Lets the subject know that the negotiator is interested in what is being said.
    f. Builds trust in the "we-they" relationship of the negotiator and subject.
4. Asking questions
    a. This is a simple way to get a clearer idea of the subject's meaning.
    b. Ask questions.
    c. Ask simple questions.
    d. Ask one question at a time. This is suggested unless asking multiple questions is done for a specific tactical purpose.

e. Ask open-ended questions to gain information.
f. Ask closed-ended questions to pinpoint specific items. This is especially effective when the negotiator is fairly sure what additional information is needed.

KNOW WHEN AND HOW TO ASK QUESTIONS

1. Can be used to obtain accurate information if done correctly.
2. Probably necessary and often helpful.
3. Pace of questions must be considered in order not to raise the subject's stress level, unless this is desired.
4. Bombarding with questions can confuse and frustrate the subject, and even, at times, the negotiator.
5. Allow sufficient time for the subject to answer the questions posed.
6. Ask in a nonthreatening and nonaccusatory tone.

DEAL EFFECTIVELY WITH SILENCE

The negotiator will often encounter silence when dealing with hostage takers, hostages, and crisis victims. Knowing how to handle the silence is very important. For some negotiators, silence is deadly. It need not be.

1. Do not assume that silence means that nothing is happening.
2. Learn to be comfortable with your feelings of being uncomfortable.
3. Use silent moments to listen more carefully for intelligence information in the background.
4. Handle silence by being silent.
5. Pay attention to what the subject is "not saying."
6. Why has the subject not said it?
7. What significance does this silence have in the overall scenario?
8. If the silence persists, you may want to reassure the subject or victim that you are still there and ready to listen if he or she wants to talk.

9. After you reassure the subject, remain quiet.
10. Insert information or empathy into silence only as actually deemed necessary.
11. Persistent silence can be broken by the negotiator carrying on both sides of the conversation as though the subject were responding. The subject may reenter the conversation just to find out what is going on. This technique requires practice and can be very effective.

UNDERSTAND CONTENT AND FEELINGS

1. Listen for both feelings and content.
2. Learn all that you can about the other person's thoughts and feelings.
3. Let the subject know some things about you, if appropriate. Self-disclosure is not always appropriate. However, revealing certain nonsensitive things about yourself may help put the other person at ease. It may make the negotiator seem more nearly human.
4. Use descriptive statements and reveal your reactions to the other person, as needed.
5. Use your own feelings, as warranted. Do not be afraid of this.
6. Note that feelings are important in communicating, and that they are always present.
7. Practice expressing your own feelings. It is not as easy as one would think. Sometimes, it is especially difficult for police officers and even negotiators.
8. Take responsibility for your feelings.
9. Use communications messages to the subject that begin with "I" rather than "you." Those beginning with "I" tend to reduce the threat to the other person. Also, use "I" rather than "we" when talking to the subject. This reinforces the "we-they" relationship and makes the current interaction appear more personal.
10. Use descriptive statements that contain feelings.
11. Be clear and specific about your feelings.

RESPOND TO THE SUBJECT EFFECTIVELY

1. Paraphrase the subject's statements to gain clarification.
2. Ask for clarification when necessary. Do not interrupt unless you must to avoid a misunderstanding.
3. Respond in a descriptive manner.
4. Do not be evaluative in your responses in order to avoid defensiveness from the subject.
5. Remember that "rightness" or "wrongness" may not be the issue.
6. Effective communication is not a contest. Unfortunately, some police negotiators think that it is and that they must "out communicate" the subject. The "win or lose" mentality is actually inappropriate here.
7. Be sure to do an assessment of needs—all needs that may present themselves.
8. Consider the needs of all involved.
9. Address issues over which the subject has actual control.
10. Deliver responses at the time that they are most important.
11. Deliver responses as soon as possible after the behavior that requires a response.
12. Assess whether the other person is ready to handle your response at this time.
13. Discuss emotional issues with as much privacy as possible.

LISTEN CAREFULLY

1. Learn and practice effective listening.
2. Strive to hear fully what the subject is saying, and what he or she might be really saying. It takes practice.
3. If possible, depending on the situation, maintain appropriate eye contact.
4. Let the subject speak freely. Do not interrupt.
5. Try to comprehend what the subject is saying even if it sounds garbled or strange.
6. During conversations with a victim or a subject, keep in mind the following:
   a. Listening is basic to successful communication.

b. Listening requires responsiveness.

c. Listening encourages expression.

d. Listening enables the listener to know more about the speaker.

e. Listening allows exploration of both feelings and content.

f. Listening helps establish trust between subject and negotiator.

g. Listening allows greater accuracy of communication.

h. Listening requires practice and is not always easy to learn.

i. Listening includes listening for content, feelings, and for points of view.

j. Listening lets the negotiator relax.

k. Attitudes and feelings may be conveyed nonverbally.

7. When you listen, remember to do the following:

a. Attend to verbal content.

b. Attend to nonverbal cues.

c. Hear and observe.

d. Attend to the feelings expressed by the subject or victim.

e. Do not think about other issues when you are listening to the subject. Hard to do? That is why you have a secondary negotiator. Let that person attend to everything else except the actual negotiations.

f. Do not listen with only "half an ear."

g. Become attuned to the speaker's verbal and nonverbal messages.

h. Note any extra emphasis the speaker places on certain words.

i. Notice the subject's speech patterns and recurring themes.

BE AWARE OF NONVERBAL MESSAGES

1. Nonverbal messages may be conveyed in the following ways. Watch and listen carefully. How many of these can be discerned over the telephone?

a. Sighing

b. Flipping through papers

c. Wincing

d. Looking around or up and down

    e. Smoking

    f. Chewing gum

    g. Yawning

    h. Tapping a finger or foot

    i. Frowning

    j. Displaying nervousness

    k. Avoiding eye contact

    l. Saying nothing

    m. Making jerky gestures

    n. Dressing sloppily

    o. Blinking rapidly

    p. Constantly looking at a clock or watch

    q. Acting bored

    r. Showing favoritism

    s. Being drunk

2. Nonverbal cues that may indicate openness:

    a. Uncrossed legs

    b. Open hands

    c. Unbuttoned coat

    d. Hands spread apart

    e. Leaning forward

    f. A willingness to speak of more personal things

    g. Appearing to accept the negotiator

3. Nonverbal cues that may indicate defensiveness:

    a. Fists closed

    b. Arms crossed in front of individual

    c. Legs crossed

    d. One leg over the chair arm

    e. Being very matter-of-fact in conversations with the negotiator

    f. Rejecting the negotiator

    g. Abruptly hanging up the telephone

4. Nonverbal cues that may indicate cooperation:

    a. Opening his or her coat

    b. Tilted head

    c. Sitting on the edge of the chair

    d. Eye contact

    e. Hand-to-face gestures

f. Leaning forward

g. A willingness to bargain

h. Keeping an agreement once reached

i. Making relevant suggestions

j. Making realistic suggestions

5. Nonverbal cues that may indicate evaluating:

   a. Head tilted

   b. Stroking chin

   c. Looking over glasses

   d. Pacing

   e. Pinching the bridge of the nose

   f. Asking for clarification

   g. Repeating conditions or instructions

   h. Asking if he or she can surrender to the negotiator

   i. Asking if the negotiator can protect him or her

   j. Asking if he or she will be handcuffed or embarrassed

6. Nonverbal cues that may indicate readiness:

   a. Hands on hips

   b. Leaning forward

   c. Confident speech patterns

   d. Moving closer to another person involved

   e. Asking for clarification

   f. Asking for protection

   g. Suggesting alternatives that are adaptive and possible

   h. Asking for help from the negotiator in obtaining additional help for self or for others

KNOW THE ROADBLOCKS
TO EFFECTIVE COMMUNICATION

1. Do not let your own feelings get in the way of understanding what the other person is trying to say.

2. Do not store up old concerns for later discussion. This is akin to the suggestion that the negotiator not bring up old demands.

3. Do not use old or saved concerns as a weapon.

4. Avoid being judgmental or critical. Avoid preaching.
5. Be sure that your responses to the subject are timely.

USE THE COMMUNICATION EXERCISES
TO PRACTICE COMMUNICATION SKILLS

1. Practice, practice, practice communication skills to develop the greatest effectiveness. It sounds easy, but is hard. This requires work to develop.
2. Now, go back and practice some more. My experience tells me that the first failures in a negotiations scenario are the communication skills of the primary negotiator. All of us, especially "cops," believe that they are communicators. Some are and some are not. Whether one is a good communicator or not depends on the skills that he or she learns and is then willing to use again and again.

Chapter 13

Planning and Preparing Equipment

It is fair to say that true professionals are distinguished from all others by the tools with which they perform their trade, by the fact that they have the needed tools for the job at hand, and by the way they maintain their tools. Perhaps more, but certainly it is no less true, for hostage and crisis negotiators. For negotiators, equipment is not only relevant to what they do, but will often be essential to their ability to perform at all. Whereas a carpenter without a hammer is only inconvenienced, the negotiator without a telephone, notebook and checklists, proper clothing, or protective gear, may be placed in imminent jeopardy and ultimately cause the demise of hostages, hostage takers, and others involved.

KEEP PERSONAL EQUIPMENT WITHIN ARM'S REACH

No one would dispute that the tactical officer without a rifle or body armor is not prepared to perform. So, also for the negotiator who attempts to negotiate without reliable equipment. In addition, the negotiator creates additional problems if he or she has not taken the time, preincident, to ponder, plan, and provide that gear that can be anticipated as critical personally and to the negotiations team.

The equipment of the negotiator can be divided into at least two distinct groups: personal gear and team gear. Some overlap of groupings may exist. However, such a listing provides a starting point for examining these needs. Refinement of equipment lists must be an ongoing responsibility of each negotiator individually, and of each negotiations team severally. Finding oneself on the "front line," absent needed material, is not the time to begin the process of equipment determination. Clearly, it is a task that is begun, within a new team, at the time of commencement of training, and by a formed team, immediately. It is hard enough to battle the elements, the topography, the "bad guys," the stress, and the frustrations of a critical incident, without also having to battle the results of poor planning and lack of preparation.

The job of the negotiator is a tough one to say the very least. Even under the best of overall conditions, the task is psychologically demanding, physically stressing, interpersonally challenging, legally frightening, and even, perhaps, career determining. Taking the time to handle potential equipment problems and needs cannot solve all of the inherent dangers in these areas. However, what such planning can do is allow all of the efforts and concentration of the negotiator to be well focused. It can be focused on the primary job at hand—that of preserving human life through the successful resolution of the critical incident. If negotiators take negotiating seriously, they must also understand the serious nature of personal and team equipment needs. Left to chance, the likelihood of disaster increases. Conversely, proper planning and care will raise the probability of positive performance and positive outcome.

REFER TO THE LIST OF RECOMMENDED PERSONAL EQUIPMENT

The following are detailed, although nonexhaustive, lists of personal and team equipment. The negotiator is encouraged to refine these lists according to need and personal style. "Having what you need rather than needing what you should have had," could be a motto for all negotiators to ensure success.

   AM/FM personal radio
   Binoculars
   Body armor
   Camp stool
   Cellular phone
   Change of clothing and underwear
   Equipment carryall kit
   Extra batteries
   First aid kit
   Flashlight
   Gun/ammunition/badge

Knife
Negotiator cap
Negotiator distinctive jacket or vest
Negotiator notebook
Nonperishable foodstuffs (e.g., trail mix, MREs, C rations)
Notepads
Observation mirror
Pens/pencils
Personal comfort items
Personal hygiene items
Portable police radio
Seasonal clothing
Small tools
Small-change money
Stethoscope
Tactical periscope
Tactical uniform
Water
Wet weather gear

ASSEMBLE AND MAINTAIN TEAM EQUIPMENT

Attention to equipment demands, as well as to maintenance, could be the difference between life and death, winning or losing, succeeding or failing, in extremely real terms. More than a mere inconvenience, the lack of forethought and planning on the part of the negotiator regarding his or her needs at the scene will be a determining factor in the overall outcome. Even the best negotiator who is well trained to perform under such circumstances as are often encountered cannot be expected to be maximally effective and thereby critically helpful if needed tools are not available.

REFER TO THE LIST OF RECOMMENDED TEAM EQUIPMENT

Additional tape recorder and tapes
Batteries in all sizes used

Cell phones
Empty cigarette packets for sending in small quantities of ciga-
    rettes
Equipment carryall, as needed
Felt-tip markers
First aid kit
Flashlights
Flip charts or newsprint
Hostage telephone system
Intrateam and interorganizational communication equipment
Loudhailer/loudspeaker/megaphone
Masking tape
Notepads
Observation mirrors
Paper towels
Pens and pencils
Phone line and reel
Plastic overlay
Public radio and television
Stethoscope
Surveillance gear
Telephone lineman's phone
Throw-in phone and padded bag
Thumbtacks or pushpins
Toilet paper
Tools
Trash bags
Water

DEVELOP AN EQUIPMENT POLICY
FOR YOUR TEAM

The following is a proposed equipment policy for negotiations
teams. Such a policy should be developed in addition to overall departmental negotiations policy. It seems appropriate that such a policy is
correctly developed and enforced by the members of the hostage negotiations team in consultation with the on-scene commander, as well
as with the approval of the chief of police.

Equipment Policy for Police Negotiations Teams

Index

Purpose

0.0. The purpose of this policy is to provide guidance to negotiators and negotiations teams regarding planning, preparation, and maintenance of personal and team equipment that may be needed during a hostage, barricaded, or suicidal incident.

0.1. It is understood by all that availability of necessary equipment and material is directly related to overall successful outcome of these critical incidents.

Guidelines

1.0. All material and equipment issued by the negotiations team to an individual negotiator shall be maintained in a high state of readiness and repair at all times. All issued gear shall be returned in good condition when the negotiator leaves the negotiations team.

2.0. All personal items that may be required by a negotiator at the scene of a critical incident will be maintained and readily available to the negotiator at all times and in a high state of readiness and repair.

Responsibilities

3.0. The responsibility for maintenance, repair, and storage of team equipment will be assigned to one team member. This team member will report periodically to the team regarding the state of readiness of all team equipment.

3.1. Although one team member will be assigned as custodian of the team equipment, all team members have a responsibility for being aware of the level of readiness of all team equipment and for reporting any deficiencies found to the negotiations team.

Equipment Availability

4.0. Each negotiator will maintain his or her personal equipment at "arm's length" while within the jurisdiction of this department.

4.1. Each negotiator will have the ability to access all team equipment whenever needed and will be aware of where all equipment is stored.

Team Equipment

5.0. A team equipment list will be maintained near the team equipment.

   5.1. All equipment listed will be checked by the equipment custodian and/or by any team member from time to time and deficiencies noted on the list.

   5.2. The custodian, upon noticing any deficiencies in the equipment or on the list, will notify the team and obtain departmental guidance regarding repair.

   5.3. Minor repairs should be made immediately by the custodian or another team member.

6.0. Team equipment shall be exercised by the team on a regular monthly basis in order to check for deficiencies and to effect repairs.

Equipment Inspections

7.0. Personal equipment shall be inspected by all team members from time to time as indicated by the team coordinator.

   7.1. Such a "showdown" will be for the purpose, and conducted in such a way, as to provide continual assistance to each team member regarding necessary and crucial supplies that may be needed.

Failure to Maintain

8.0. Failure to maintain personal equipment at an acceptable high state of readiness and repair will be sufficient grounds for removal of the officer from the negotiations team.

   8.1. Failure to act in a competent manner as custodian of team equipment shall be sufficient grounds for removal of the officer from the negotiations team.

   8.2. Failure of any negotiations team member to notice, note, report, take action relevant to repairs, or to apprise himself or herself of the state of readiness of any and all team equipment, shall be grounds for removal of the officer from the negotiations team.

8.3. Removal of an officer from the team due to violations listed in 8.0, 8.1, or 8.2 will be decided by the members of the negotiations team acting as a whole or by the senior administrative officer of the department.

Callout

9.0. It shall be the responsibility of each team member to bring all personal equipment to the scene of any hostage, barricaded, or suicidal incident.

9.1. It shall be the responsibility of all team members to ensure that all team equipment is transported to the scene of a critical incident.

9.2. Each team member, on callout, should inquire concerning the disposition of team equipment, and as necessary, take personal responsibility for transporting team equipment to the scene.

9.3. Under certain conditions, when the tactical team is deploying, and the negotiations team equipment has not yet been deployed, the tactical commander and/or members of the tactical team will bring all identified negotiations team equipment to the incident scene.

9.4. All negotiations team equipment will be so marked as to be readily identifiable for deployment by the tactical unit as necessary. Such markings might include bright-colored duct tape or similar type markings.

9.5. All negotiations team equipment transported to the scene of a critical incident by the tactical unit will be delivered to the on-scene commander or to the senior negotiator available at the scene.

9.6. It will be the responsibility of the negotiations team leader/coordinator to notify the tactical commander concerning the markings used to identify negotiations team equipment for tactical deployment.

Deployment of Equipment at the Scene

10.0. Deployment of any equipment at the scene, within the inner cordon/perimeter or to the stronghold/target area, will be the sole responsibility of the tactical unit.

10.1. A negotiator may be assigned to the tactical unit to assist in deployment of the throw-in phone and phone line to the stronghold/target area. This assigned negotiator will be assisted in the deployment of the phone and line by members of the tactical unit and will be under the direct authority of the tactical commander or his or her agent.

10.2. Under such conditions, assignment of the negotiator to the tactical team shall be the sole responsibility of the negotiations coordinator/team leader.

This policy should be modified and adapted to specific team needs. The team itself should be responsible for developing these guidelines.

Chapter 14

Heeding the Laws of Hostage and Crisis Negotiations

Successful hostage and crisis negotiations require that negotiators possess both talent and skill. Development of the necessary skills takes time, effort, and commitment. More is required than the mere recitation of words and phrases. The following list is not intended to replace hands-on training, and reading the list will not a negotiator make. However, even with the intentional humor, these reminders may serve as the basis for a complete negotiations course. Each covers specific elements important to the police negotiator and is designed to serve as a point of departure for discussion and clarification. Many of the laws are derived and adapted from negotiations teams and team philosophies from all over the world. Use them wisely.

1. Reason rather than react.
2. Innovate, adapt, prevail.
3. Contain, isolate, evaluate, negotiate; evaluate, negotiate; evaluate, negotiate.
4. Never water barren trees.
5. When you find yourself in a circle, go for the feelings.
6. If your gut says no, don't go.
7. Develop your skills so that mistakes are what other people make.
8. Maximize the utilization of available resources.
9. Negotiate for as long as a life is worth.
10. Negotiators don't command, and commanders don't negotiate.
11. Add nothing for "what it's worth."
12. Knowing what to stay out of is as important as knowing what to get into.

13. Care about your other negotiators. Support one another.
14. Develop arrows for your quiver.
15. Seek to understand, then to be understood. (Stephen R. Covey)
16. Speak softly and carry big schtick.
17. Mouth marines do it orally.
18. If the train is not going where you want to go, get off.
19. To assume anything makes an "Ass" of "U" and "Me."
20. Don't hate your enemies. It will cloud your judgment.
21. Learn to be comfortable being uncomfortable.
22. Silence is golden. Learn to shut up and strike gold.
23. Never retreat. Just attack in a different direction.
24. The only failure is nonresolution.
25. Hostage negotiations is a team effort; not an individual event.
26. Individuals make the best team players.
27. Pass the buck regularly.
28. All things come to those who wait if they work like hell while they wait.
29. Just because they're crazy doesn't mean they're stupid.
30. Bumbling isn't always bad.
31. Acceptance does not imply agreement.
32. Shotguns scatter; precision matters.
33. "There are no such things as great men or great women; only extraordinary challenges that ordinary people are forced, by circumstances, to meet." (Admiral W. F. "Bull" Halsey, paraphrased)
34. Change behavior. Attitudes will follow.
35. Most people live in their gut.
36. Never meet force head-on.
37. Negotiators have one mouth and two ears. The operational implications are obvious.
38. "If you're going to learn to play the game, you've got to learn to play it right." (paraphrased from "The Gambler" by Kenny Rogers)
39. "It is a wise man who uses words before resorting to arms." (Terrence Publius)
40. "[M]en, when they receive good from whence they expect evil, feel all the more indebted to their benefactor." (Machiavelli, *The Prince*)
41. Semper Ubi Sub Ubi (Always wear underwear).

42. "I am not what I think I am. I am not what you think I am. I am what I think you think I am." (George Herbert Mead)
43. "In order to remain helpful, we must remain effective." (Dr. Edward S. Rosenbluh)
44. Hostage and crisis negotiations is not a "wait and see" option.
45. Downtime is work time.
46. Train as if your life and the lives of others depended on it; someday it will.
47. The more you know, the more you have.
48. Something for nothing has little value.
49. If at first you don't succeed, the hell with it.
50. Successful hostage negotiations require some common sense and a lot of uncommon sense.
51. Needs + Wants + Needs = Success.
52. Don't sell used cars.
53. Defuse before you debrief.
54. Many have the time to do it over; the negotiator must do it right the first time.
55. The mark of the professional is the condition and availability of his or her tools.
56. Nothing works all the time with all people.
57. Gather intelligence intelligently.
58. Winning isn't everything; it's the only thing.
59. There is no such thing as a good loser.
60. Suicide has nothing to do with death.
61. The buck stops somewhere else.
62. Don't bullshit a bullshitter.
63. Avoid lying.
64. If you do lie, don't get caught.
65. Lie only about big things; never about little things.
66. Negotiators seldom lie. They just engage in tactical expressions.
67. Deliver what you promise.
68. Perception is in the eye of the beholder.
69. Some things are not as easy as they seem; some are.
70. Ask them to come out.
71. Speak of "suicide."
72. Words are the lifeblood of the negotiator.
73. Negotiators can ill-afford the imprecision of language.

74. Jargon is spoken by jargs.
75. Control by not controlling.
76. Courtesy costs you nothing.
77. Determine, diagnose, dispose.
78. Plan well. Then, plan again.
79. The major virtue in telling the truth is that you don't have to remember what you've said. (My mother of blessed memory)
80. Negotiators are real cops, too.
81. Negotiations are like Crock-Pot cooking; it takes time.
82. "Goodwill" is illusive.
83. First of all, do no harm.
84. No matter how thin you make your pancakes, they always have two sides.
85. Persons will never be left the same as you found them.
86. Hostages deserve our concern.
87. Bad guys are people too.
88. Crazy people are doing the best that they can.
89. "Deadlines are the sand traps on the golf course of life." ("Snoopy" in *Peanuts* by Charles Schultz)
90. It is better to take your time than to take a life.
91. Slow everything down.
92. To thine own self be true.
93. Visualize a successful resolution.
94. Have a reason.
95. Don't let your opening be your closing.
96. Make haste slowly.
97. Buck-passing is an art form.
98. Be an agent of reality.
99. Rapport unlocks the door.
100. A negotiator must be: hard of hearing; not too smart; somewhat of a bumbler; a little ignorant; unexciting; and "normal" as well.
101. Boring is good.
102. Cover your assets.
103. Demands are the basis of bargaining.
104. Sow the seeds of doubt and risk.
105. Deal only with the problems; and everything is a problem.
106. Nothing is so important as that which is trivial.
107. Think "intell."

108. Beware of the "spiral of excitement."
109. "No" to "No."
110. A negotiated resolution can only occur between two perceived equals.
111. Difficult negotiations take a while; miracles take a little longer.
112. Don't shoot with bullets.
113. Don't promise if you can't do it.
114. The Goldilocks rule: "It can't be too hot or too cold; it can't be too much or too little; it must be just right." (McGowan)
115. If you don't understand, don't say that you do.
116. Crystallize your objective.
117. Create social expectations.
118. Create a "winning vision."
119. Concentrate on "now," not on "next."
120. "What if?" it.
121. Prove life.
122. Bank agreements.
123. Build the positive. Level the negative.
124. Hot wash up always.
125. Don't surrender to surrenders.
126. Use deaf and dumb interpreters.
127. Invest in emotions.
128. Always "AB."
129. Silent running.
130. Check the time.
131. Imperturbability is boring.
132. Train to win; prepare to lose.
133. Be soft on people; hard on problems. (R. Fisher et al.)
134. Go for interests; avoid positions.
135. Seek alternatives.
136. Use objective standards.
137. Don't call me; I'll call you.
138. Try to resolve each situation; acknowledge that you may not resolve every situation.
139. Hear what isn't being said.
140. Luck = Preparation + Opportunity.
141. You can go anywhere if you have the time.
142. An authority on negotiations is someone who has guessed right more than once.

143. Don't judge if you feel no compassion.
144. Trust in God, but tie your camel tight.
145. Time will dispose of the trivial.
146. Negotiators are persons who make waves, and then convince the taker that they are the only ones who can save the ship.
147. It's not over until it's over.
148. Plan your surrender plan.
149. Hook 'em hard.
150. You can learn many good things from a bad situation.
151. You must do more than talk the talk. You must know how to walk the walk.
152. Keep your friends close; keep your mayo jar even closer.
153. Keep breathing.
154. Divert force.
155. Use the subject's strength against him or her.
156. Know when the sky is falling and when it isn't.
157. Never underestimate the power of stupid people in large groups.
158. Persistence is omnipotent.
159. A soft answer turns away wrath.

Appendix I

Useful Forms and Illustrations
for the Negotiator in the Field

DEBRIEFING SHEET

Name given to hostage/crisis situation:
Service number: Type of situation:
Date of situation:
Location:
Time team called:
#1:   Date of HNT debriefing:
#2:   Date of SWAT debriefing:
#3:
#4:
#5:
Other negotiators:
Suspect(s):
Age, race, sex:
Hostages held:
Hostages released:
Family members held:
Family members released:
Deaths:
Injuries:
Motive:
Time event began:
Time event ended:
Total event time:
Time negotiations began:
Time negotiations ended:
Communication method:
Method of resolution: Diagnosis:
Total negotiating time:
Suspect clothing:
Suspect criminal history:
Suspect weapon capability:
Rounds fired:
Targets:

Primary substantive demands:
Other suspect demands:
Demands met:
SWAT deployment:
Criminal charges:
Disposition:
Pled to:
Sentence received:
Other pertinent information about this incident:

INTELLIGENCE REPORT

Instructions: Use one report per person interviewed.

You Are Going to See

Name:
Phone:
Address:
Relationship: The person to be interviewed by you is (what):
    To (whom):

Individual Description of: _____ Hostage taker _____ Hostage

Name:
Phone:
Home address:
Work address:
Occupation:
Skills:
Military service:
    1. Branch:
    2. Rank:
    3. Problems:
Race:
Sex:
Date of birth:
Age:
Height:
Weight:
Hair color:
Eye color:
Driver's license number:
Social security number:
Alias:
Nickname:
Languages spoken:
Vehicles owned:
    License number:
Vehicles used:
    License number:
Type of clothing worn and description:
Distinguishing characteristics:

Historical Background

1. Criminal history:
2. Psychological history:
3. Medical history:
4. Family background:
5. Close friends:
6. Hobbies and special interests:
7. Significant events leading to this situation:

Activities on This Date

Information Linking Victims or Hostages with the Hostage Taker

Physical Description of the Immediate Area and of the Stronghold Including All Entrances and Exits

Weapons Possessed

Additional Information

Photograph Attached: _____ yes _____ no

Interviewer:
ID number:
Unit:

CHECKLIST FOR NEGOTIATIONS TECHNIQUES

Do	**Notes**
Have a good opening statement.	
Be empathetic.	
Be credible.	
Have good voice control.	
Good stress tolerance.	
Gather intelligence.	
Establish a psychological profile.	
Listen actively.	
Pause to listen.	
Encourage ventilation.	
Use self-disclosure carefully.	
Be flexible.	
Nurture the escape potential.	
Ask open-ended questions.	
Be reassuring.	
Make the hostage taker feel responsible for the hostages.	
List demands accurately.	
Pass off responsibility.	
Talk in terms of *"we,"* meaning the negotiator and the subject.	
Talk on the level of the hostage taker.	
Use reflective responses.	
Acknowledge the hostage taker's feelings.	
Use reassuring phrases.	
Give positive approval.	
Keep the subject in a decision-making mode.	

Do Not

Interrupt the hostage taker.

Ask superfluous questions.

Be argumentative.

Make decisions for the subject.

Make promises that you cannot keep.

Use trigger or "bullet" words.

Say *"we,"* meaning the negotiator and the police.

Irritate the subject.

Volunteer information.

Talk too much.

Get mad or irritated.

Make assumptions.

Get angry with command.

Be authoritarian.

Be tough except if planned.

Be too soft unless planned.

Be defensive.

Notes

HOSTAGE/VICTIM WORKSHEET

Instructions: Use one worksheet for each hostage or victim.

Hostage Number:

Name:

Nationality:

Occupation:

Address: City/state/zip:

Religion:

Height:	Weight:	Sex:
Eyes:	Build:	Hair:
Race:	Glasses:	Scars:
Other:		

Clothing

Shirt:	Pants/dress:
Jacket:	Shoes:
Hat:	Coat:

Other clothing items:

Medical history:

Medical needs: Times required:

Psychological tendencies:

Primary language:
Other languages spoken:
Other related information:

FIELD DIAGNOSTIC WORKSHEET

Date:
Service number:
Name of incident:
Name of subject profiled:
Profiler:

Diagnosis/Profile

List the specific characteristics observed in the subject, or related to the subject, that ultimately justify the above diagnosis.

1.
2.
3.
4.
5.
6.
7.
8.
9.
10.

Proposed Negotiations Strategies and Goals
Based on the Primary Diagnosis

1.
2.
3.
4.
5.

Notes for Primary Negotiator

INTELLIGENCE-GATHERING FORMAT
FOR FIRST RESPONDERS

Subject(s):

    1. Identity:
    2. Description:

Possible motive:

Hostage information:

    Hostage number one:
    Hostage number two:
    Hostage number three:

Weapons information:

Level of violence displayed or threatened:

Structural details of stronghold:

Position of all officers:

Location of noncombatants within the inner perimeter:

Map/sketch of stronghold:

Map/sketch of incident area:

QUICK STRATEGY WORKSHEET

Name of Subject: _____ Date: _____ Time: _____

☐ Incident just began.
☐ Ongoing incident: _____hours

Suicidal?   ____Yes   ____ No   ____Talk only   ____ Attempt

Who is he or she? (What do we know about the subject? name, rank, and serial number)	What are the subject's concerns? (specific expressed fears, needs, wants, and concerns)

Will come out of _____
Will not come out because _____

How Do We Meet the Specific Concern?

Strategy

Ploys

NEGOTIATIONS CHECKLIST

Checklist initiated by:

Incident

1. Location:
2. What happened:
3. Time:

Injuries To

1. Police:
2. Hostages:
3. Hostage takers:
4. Bystanders:
5. Others:

Contact

1. Who initiated contact:
2. When:
3. How:
4. Demands:

Location

1. Hostages:
2. Hostage takers:
3. Police:
4. Bystanders:

Building

1. Floor plans:
2. Exits and entrances:
3. Telephones:
4. Radios/televisions/computers:

Weapons

1. Handguns:
2. Rifles/shotguns:
3. Explosives:
4. Chemicals:
5. Biologicals:

6. WMD:
7. Other:

Hostage Takers

1. How many:
2. Positive identification:
3. Description:
4. Clothing:
5. Criminal history:
6. Other records checks:
7. Medical information:
8. Psychological information:
9. Family information:
10. Friends:
11. Witnesses:

Hostages

1. Positive identification:
2. Description:
3. Clothing:
4. Number of hostages:
5. How secured by HT:
6. Injuries:
7. Medical information:
8. Psychological information:

Deadlines

1. Time limits:
2. Ultimatums:
3. Demands:
4. Deal breakers:

Notes and Additional Comments and Specific Information

DETAILED INTELLIGENCE REPORT

Subject number:

Date:

Service number:

Subject name:

Sex:

Date of birth:

Address/city/state:

Also known as:

Photo of subject available: ___ yes ___ no

Primary negotiator:

Length of negotiations:

Hostages/names/sex/age/relationship to hostage taker:

Barricade incident or hostage situation:

If hostage situation, are hostage taker substantive demands:

1. Reasonable
2. Exorbitant
3. Weird
4. None
5. Other

Medical information:

Psychological information:

Suicide information:

Military background:

Substance abuse information:

Marital relationships and conflicts:

Childhood history:

Religion and religious practices and beliefs:

Personality traits:

Criminal history:

Behavior at this scene:

Diagnosis and profile:

Negotiation strategies:

1. Positive
2. Negative
3. Ploys
4. Subject will come out if
5. Subject will not come out because

Additional notes:

MENTAL STATUS EXAMINATION

For use by hostage negotiations team mental health consultant or intelligence coordinator.

Name of subject: _____

Date form completed: _____ by: _____

Attitude and General Behavior

Physical	within normal limits	disheveled	untidy	unkept
Cooperation	WNL	fair	poor	
General manner	WNL	mistrustful	suspicious	antagonistic
Activity	negativistic	defiant	preoccupied	
	motor retardation	hyperactivity	stereotype	mannerisms
	tics	echolalia	echopraxia	perseveration
	compulsion			

Stream of Talk and Mental Activity

Accessibility	indifferent	self-absorbed	inaccessible
Productivity	voluble	circumstantial	flight of ideas
	under-productive	retarded	mute
Thought progression	illogical	irrelevant	incoherent
	verbigeration	blocking	
Neologisms			

Emotional Reactions

Quality of affect	WNL	elation	exhilaration	exaltation
	euphoria	mild depression	moderate depression	
	severe depression	apprehension	fear	anxiety
	emotional instability			

Appropriateness of affect	incongruity with thought content	emotional deterioration
	ambivalence	

Content of Thoughts

Thinking disorder	phobias	obsessive ideas
	psycho-somatic complaints	persecutory trend
	grandiose ideas	depressive delusions
	nihilistic delusions	hypochondriac ideas
	ideas of unreality	deprivation of thought
	delusions of influence	autistic thinking
	ideas of reference	
Perceptive dis-orders	auditory hallucinations	illusions
	visual halluci-nations	olfactory hallucinations
	tactile halluci-nations	reflex hallucinations
	hypnagogic hallucinations	psychomotor hallucinations

Sensorium and General Knowledge

Disorders of con-sciousness	confusion	clouding	dream state
	delirium	stupor	
Disorders of apperception	mild	severe	
Disorders of orientation	time	place	person

Disorders of personal identification and memory	general amnesia		
	circumscribed amnesia	confabulation	
	retrospective falsification	hyperamnesia	
Disorders of retention and immediate recall	mild	severe	
Disorders of counting and calculation	mild	severe	
Disorders of reading	mild	severe	
Disorders of writing	mild	severe	
Disorders in school and general knowledge	mild	severe	
Disorders in attention, concentration, and thinking capacity	mild	severe	
Disorders in intelligence inconsistent with education	mild	severe	
Disorders in judgment	mild	severe	
Disorders in insight	mild	severe	
Suicidality	mild	moderate	severe

Summary of Mental Status Examination

- Mental status examination essentially negative
- Disturbance in attitude and general behavior
- Disturbance in stream of mental activity
- Disturbance in emotional reaction
- Disturbance in mental trend—content of thought
- Disturbance in sensorium, mental grasp, and capacity

Suggested Negotiations Guidelines
Based on Mental Status Examination

Use:
Avoid:
More information needed about:
"Bullet words":
Expected problems:
Additional suggestions to negotiations team:
Is the actor suicidal?

THINK TANK DIAGNOSTIC WORKSHEET

Date:
Situation:

Subject's name:
Sex: Age:
Address: City/state:

Negotiator: Department:

Hostage(s):   Sex(es):
Age(s):   Relationship(s):

Demands of the hostage taker:

__ None   __ Reasonable   __ Exorbitant   __ Weird   __ Other

Medical background: Source:

Marital background: Source:

Military background: Source:

Childhood background: Source:

Criminal history: Source:

Personality traits: Source:

Behavioral characteristics at scene: Source:

Suicidal ideations or behavior: Source:

Provisional diagnosis: Source:

Negotiations strategies based on the above information:

Members of the think tank:

Command post located at: Tactical support:

This form was completed by: Identification number:

QUESTIONS TO BE ANSWERED BY THE THINK TANK

1. Why do you think the subject is really holding hostages, aside from the stated reason?
2. What does the subject really want?
3. What are the interests of the subject?
4. What alternatives do you think the subject has?
5. What does the subject think that he or she can do if he or she decides not to negotiate with us?
6. How important to the subject is the relationship that he or she has with:
   a. the hostages?
   b. other hostage takers?
   c. the negotiator?
   d. with others that are important in his or her life?
7. Does the subject perceive the negotiator as being sincere in wanting to develop a good relationship with him or her?
8. How can communication between the negotiator and subject be more effective and efficient?
9. How important is effective communication to the subject?
10. What negotiating options are available to both the negotiator and to the subject?
11. Does the subject think that the negotiator is presenting accurate, fair, and truthful information and alternatives?
12. If not, how can the negotiator do a better job in this area?
13. Does the subject present accurate, fair, and truthful information?
14. How important to the subject are the promises he or she made to the negotiator?
15. How does the subject perceive the commitments made by the negotiator?
16. Does the subject have trouble making commitments?
17. What is the subject really getting from the process of holding hostages or detaining others?
18. What does the subject see as the disadvantages of holding hostages or of detaining others?
19. What does the subject see as the disadvantages of releasing the hostages or the others that are being detained?
20. What does the subject see as the advantages of releasing the hostages or the others that are being detained?

LETHALITY SCALE

	O Points	1 Point	2 Points	3 Points	4 Points	Total
Age, male	0-12 yrs.		13-44 yrs.	45-64 yrs.	65 and up	
Age, female	0-12 yrs.	13-44 yrs.	45 and up			
Personal resources available	Good	Fair		Poor		
Current stress	Low		Medium		High	
Marital status	Married, children	Married, no children		Widowed or single	Divorced	
Current psychological functioning	Stable		Unstable			
Other problems or symptoms	Absent		Present			
Communication channels	Open		Blocked			
Physical condition	Good	Fair			Poor	
Suicide by close family member	No		Yes			
Depressed or agitated currently	No				Yes	
Prior suicidal behavior by subject	No		Yes			

(continued)

(continued)

	O Points	1 Point	2 Points	3 Points	4 Points	Total
Reactions by signifi-cant others to the needs of the subject	Helpful			Not helpful		
Current financial stress	Absent		Present			
Suicidal plan of the subject	Has none	Plan with few de-tails	Subject has selected the means for suicide		Subject has a highly spe-cific plan for suicide	
Occupation of subject	Non-help-ing pro-fession or other oc-cupation	MD, den-tist, attor-ney, or helping profes-sional	Psychia-trist, po-lice offi-cer, or unem-ployed			
Residence	Rural	Suburban	Urban			
Living arrange-ments	Lives with others				Lives alone	
Time of the year this incident is occurring		Spring				
Day of the week this incident is occurring		Sunday or Wednes-day	Monday			
Recent oc-currence of serious ar-guments with spouse or signifi-cant other	No	Yes				

(continued)

(continued)

Recently, the subject's significant other was:	The focus of a disappointment	Lost to the subject in some significant way	
			Total Points

Name of subject:
Date and time scale completed:
Name of negotiator completing this scale:
Comments and action notes:

Criteria

Minimal risk (0-15 points)   _____

Low risk (16-30 points)   _____

Medium risk (31-46 points)   _____

High risk (47-60 points)   _____

Directions for Use: Circle response in appropriate row and column. Place points from top of column in the far right column. Sum all scores under total points and match with total criteria. Scale can be run multiple times on same subject as more information becomes available.

(*Source:* Dr. Edward S. Rosenbluh. Reprinted with permission.)

COMMAND POST STRUCTURE EXAMPLE

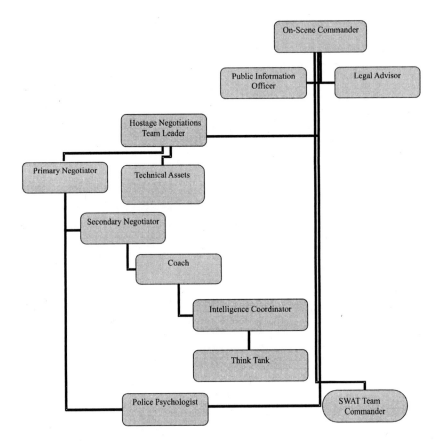

THE CRISIS CUBE

Figure A1.1 is an illustration of the crisis cube. The crisis cube is a three-dimensional representation of how a crisis develops and might be managed. A discussion of the crisis cube may be found in *The Elements of Crisis Intervention,* Second Edition (Greenstone and Leviton, 2002, p. 2).

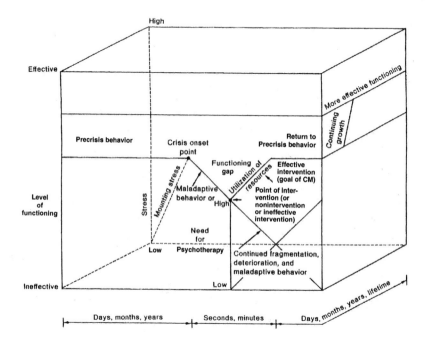

FIGURE A1.1. Crisis Cube. Copyright 2002 by James L. Greenstone.

Appendix II

Practice Using Negotiations Exercises

Following is a coordinated training scenario utilizing multiple parts that are all related. All trainees should receive the *Training Scenario*. All others should receive their own part. Negotiators should receive the *Training Scenario* only. The total package can be modified to meet local training needs. Each of the separate parts can be played by separate actors or by one actor providing all of the information for each of the parts, if asked. Information can be provided face-to-face or on the telephone, or both. The hostage taker should have access to the entire scenario package so that he or she can make proper comments consistent with the scenario and so that he or she will know what information will be available about them.

Each actor's part is set up so that if the information-gatherer asks the correct questions, the answers will be available if that actor has that specific information. If not, he or she will tell the trainee that the information about which he or she asked is not available. No information is given voluntarily by the actor. If the trainee asks the correct questions, and if the information is available from that specific actor, the actor will provide the information to the trainee. If not, the information will not be provided. The purpose here is to train negotiators to ask the necessary questions if they want certain information. They should not rely on information being provided gratuitously by the informant. In the field, however, we know that such information may be obtained in this gratuitous way. Also, negotiators gathering intelligence are encouraged to use the intelligence formats provided in Appendix I to assist them in this endeavor.

Real time should be used when utilizing this scenario. However, some abbreviations can be made as needed.

The *Simulation Exercises* are provided to assist in short training periods and for crisis-intervention training. Each will help to sharpen skills of the negotiator even though they do not specifically reference hostage situations. All parts are provided. The victims should receive only their parts. The interveners should receive theirs and be instructed to remain in the role throughout the intervention attempt.

GROUND RULES

In all training scenarios and simulations, ground rules should be established preintervention to avoid the possibilities of both physical and psychological injuries. These might include, but are not limited to, the following:

1. No firearms or ammunition in the scenario.
2. Role-players should remain in role at all times until the scenario is stopped by the person in charge of the exercise. This person is often known as "exercise control."
3. In addition to coming out of role as directed by the exercise control, role-players should come out of role if the role that they are playing happens to be very close to a real-life, unresolved conflict in their own life, or if they have made a mistake so inconsistent with the role that they cannot recover within the confines of the scenario. Staying in the role is very important for training purposes.
4. Role-players will not deviate from the assigned role without specific permission of the exercise control.
5. Role-players will not invent circumstances or play pranks on the negotiator trainees except as consistent with the scenario. Seriousness is important.
6. Trainees will not act toward the actors in ways that are inconsistent with the scenario or with the way in which they would handle a similar situation in real life negotiations.
7. For safety reasons, no pyrotechnics will be used in any of the scenarios.
8. In extended scenarios, actors' personal comfort and subsistence will be provided regardless of what is yielded by the negotiations.
9. If tactical units are used, they must play by the same rules as all others involved.
10. Immediate critique should follow all interventions and extended scenarios.

TRAINING SCENARIO

At approximately 0700, dispatch received a call from Mr. and Mrs. Smith at 4900 Summit, Your City. They reported hearing what they thought might be gunshots and loud noises from the house next to theirs at 4902 Summit. They reported hearing glass breaking, loud voices, and they were concerned about what might be happening to their neighbor whose last name is Jones. They said that they went next door to check on their neighbor but when they rang the doorbell, they were met with loud shouting from inside the house telling them to go away or that the person inside would kill them and commit suicide. They heard more of what they thought were gunshots but they were not endangered. They heard a window break in the house as well as some loud bumping noises. The Smiths retreated to their home and called the police.

The first-response officer arrived at approximately 0710 and attempted to contact Jones. After knocking several times on the door and ringing the bell, the officer was told by the person inside the house to go away and not to come back. The person repeated that the police were not needed and that everything would be taken care of. The officer heard loud noises, breaking glass, and what might have been gunshots. The person in the house would not come to the door. Threats continued that anyone who tried to enter the house would be killed. With that statement, several shots were fired through the front door, barely missing the officer. At that point, the officer retreated to call for assistance.

At 0730, the SWAT team was mobilized and the hostage and crisis negotiations team was put on alert. At 0800, the SWAT team arrived and secured the scene. Evacuation of surrounding houses was accomplished and the command post was set up.

The hostage and crisis negotiations team was mobilized and told to report directly to the command post at 4902 Summit and to approach from the west. The hostage and crisis negotiations team arrived on scene at approximately 0900 and began to set up.

It is now approximately 0915.

Hostage Taker/Barricaded Subject

You are a very depressed individual who has just learned that you have terminal cancer. You have only a few months to live. You were divorced six months ago in what was a very bitter situation with your ex-spouse. You loved your spouse very much and you cannot understand the bitterness. You love your two children, Susan and James, very much but they have moved to another state and you do not know how to reach them. You know that your ex had something to do with this. You are about to be fired from your job because of your sloppy appearance and absences from work. You are seeing a psychiatrist and your minister, but nothing seems to help. No matter what you do, the world is closing in around you and it is too much to continue to face. You do not have any hostages or detainees with you, but the police do not know that. You do have a gun, a .357 magnum, fully loaded, and you are seriously thinking about killing yourself. It is better than dying a painful death due to cancer. You would like help, but you do not think that help is possible for you and fight the ideas of help if suggested by the negotiator. Your depression is severe and it takes you a long time to respond to the negotiator. You would like to trust the negotiator, but you do not know if you can.

Note to role-player: Play this role according to and through your own personality. Go with whatever seems to flow from the role as you get into it. If the negotiator seems to be doing a good job and you feel that you would normally respond to such an attempt, then respond to the negotiator. On the other hand, if the negotiator is off the track, do not respond to him or her. Let the negotiator do the work but do not purposefully hold out if you feel within you that the negotiator is getting through to you.

Remember to go with your own feelings. This simulation will continue for several hours.

First-Response Officer

Read very carefully: This is the role that you will play in this simulation. Please use only the information provided in these instructions and in the scenario sheet. The information provided is what you will provide to the interrogators/interviewers who will talk with you at some time during the simulation. Provide *only,* I repeat *only* the information given to you. Provide this information *only* in response to specific questions about these items. This is very important. *Do not volunteer any information.* Answer questions only. **If the interviewer does not ask the specific questions to get your specific answers, make up answers to his or her questions in accordance with your understanding of the overall scenario.** The training of an interviewer is dependent on him or her knowing what questions to ask to simulation participants and your willingness to stick to your role. Under no circumstances are you to make the scenario any harder or less realistic than it is. Stick to your role at all times. Thanks!

1. *Description of subject:* None. You are unable to see the subject. Only one voice is heard and you will be told if it is a male or female voice. Mrs. Smith said that the subject is approximately forty-nine-years old and attractive. She does not know how tall the subject is but said that the subject is average.
2. *Criminal background:* No criminal history found.
3. *Mental illness history:* No information.
4. *Medical history:* No information.
5. *Family background:* Apparently lives alone according to Mrs. Smith. Has other family members living in town. Mrs. Smith doesn't think Jones is currently married. No trouble before. The two families were not close.

6. *Close relationships:* May be family members and an ex-spouse living in town. Jones had few visitors according to Mr. Smith.
7. *Significant events in the subject's life:* No information.
8. *Activities of subject today:* Mr. Smith said that when Jones drove into his driveway last night, Mr. Smith was in his own front yard. Jones usually waves to him and says, "Hello." Mr. Smith tried to speak to Jones but Jones ignored him and went directly into the house. Mr. Smith thought that this was strange.
9. *Information on victims or hostages:* Not sure if anyone else is in the house with the subject. Mrs. Smith said that when they went to check on Jones that Jones kept yelling something about "him" and "them."
10. *Physical description including entrances, exits, and floor plan of barricaded area or stronghold:* Single-family dwelling. Front and back door. One-story house.

Close, Intimate Friend to the Subject (Opposite-Sex Friend)

Read very carefully: This is the role that you will play in this simulation. Please use only the information provided in these instructions and in the scenario sheet. The information provided is what you will provide to the interrogators/interviewers who will talk with you at some time during the simulation. Provide *only,* I repeat *only* the information given to you. Provide this information *only* in response to specific questions about these items. This is very important. *Do not volunteer any information.* Answer questions only. **If the interviewer does not ask the specific questions to get your specific answers, make up answers to his or her questions in accordance with your understanding of the overall scenario.** The training of an interviewer is dependent on him or her knowing what questions to ask to simulation participants and your willingness to stick to your role. Under no circumstances are you to make the scenario any harder or less realistic than it is. Stick to your role at all times. Thanks!

11. *Description of subject:* Forty-nine years old. White. Good-looking but very haggard-looking today. Lost a lot of weight recently. Very thin and old-looking now.
12. *Criminal background:* No information.
13. *Mental illness history:* Has been seeing a minister and a psychiatrist since learning of the terminal cancer. Very worried and getting more and more depressed.
14. *Medical history:* No information.
15. *Family background:* Has two children who are grown. Was married for twenty-five years and devoted to the family. Upset very much

when kids left and moved to another state. Does not know how to contact them.

16. *Close relationships:* We are very close.
17. *Significant events in the subject's life:* No information.
18. *Activities of subject today:* Left here two days ago and has not been heard from since. I tried to make contact at work yesterday but line was always busy. This is very unlike Jones not to talk to me every day.
19. *Information on victims or hostages:* No information.
20. *Physical description including entrances, exits, and floor plan of barricaded area or stronghold:* One-story, single-family dwelling. Nicely furnished. Two bedrooms in the back with living room in the front of the house. Backdoor is off of the kitchen.

Doctor/Psychiatrist

Read very carefully: This is the role that you will play in this simulation. Please use only the information provided in these instructions and in the scenario sheet. The information provided is what you will provide to the interrogators/interviewers who will talk with you at some time during the simulation. Provide *only,* I repeat *only* the information given to you. Provide this information *only* in response to specific questions about these items. This is very important. *Do not volunteer any information.* Answer questions only. **If the interviewer does not ask the specific questions to get your specific answers, make up answers to his or her questions in accordance with your understanding of the overall scenario.** The training of an interviewer is dependent on him or her knowing what questions to ask to simulation participants and your willingness to stick to your role. Under no circumstances are you to make the scenario any harder or less realistic than it is. Stick to your role at all times. Thanks!

1. *Description of subject:* Forty-nine-year-old Caucasian suffering from severe depression. Some suicidal ideations but without psychotic features. Some paranoia about relationships with ex-spouse and with boss and about people being out to get the subject in vague, nondescript ways. Has recently been diagnosed as having terminal cancer. Feels that this should not be happening. Has been unable to sleep at night, has feelings of hopelessness and helplessness, is not eating regularly, and has lost fifty pounds in the past six weeks. Goes out less and less and is withdrawing from friends and family. Has lost interest in usual activities and has been absent from work so much that there is a danger of being fired. Is oriented to time and space and overall sensorium is clear. I suggested that the

subject be on some mild medication for the depression. Subject refused. Came in to see me last week and is supposed to see again the day after tomorrow. Is probably suicidal and should be back in therapy as soon as possible. Has a lot of anger held inside and could explode on self or others. Rapport with this subject is important as well as some immediate hope for the future.

2. *Criminal background:* No criminal history found.
3. *Mental illness history:* No previous history of mental illness to my knowledge. Only the current episode. I suspect that subject has experienced similar crises before.
4. *Medical history:* Generally, in good physical health. Weight loss is of great concern and is part of the depression. Recent diagnosis of cancer.
5. *Family background:* Large family. Brothers and sisters killed in accident. Feels somehow responsible for their deaths. Low self-esteem secondary to parent's divorce. School life and early adulthood unremarkable.
6. *Close relationships:* Loved ex-spouse very much. Cannot understand why ex-spouse is so bitter and resentful now. Current friend of the opposite sex is strong source of support.
7. *Significant events in the subject's life:* Death of brothers and sisters. Diagnosis of terminal cancer. Divorce and resulting bitterness.
8. *Activities of subject today:* Called me earlier but I was in session and could not speak with the subject. I tried to return the call but could not reach the subject.
9. *Information on victims or hostages:* No information.
10. *Physical description including entrances, exits, and floor plan of barricaded area or stronghold:* No information.

Friend of Subject

Read very carefully: This is the role that you will play in this simulation. Please use only the information provided in these instructions and in the scenario sheet. The information provided is what you will provide to the interrogators/interviewers who will talk with you at some time during the simulation. Provide *only,* I repeat *only* the information given to you. Provide this information *only* in response to specific questions about these items. This is very important. *Do not volunteer any information.* Answer questions only. **If the interviewer does not ask the specific questions to get your specific answers, make up answers to his or her questions in accordance with your understanding of the overall scenario.** The training of an interviewer is dependent on him or her knowing what questions to ask to simulation participants and your willingness to stick to your role. Under no circumstances are you to make the scenario any harder or less realistic than it is. Stick to your role at all times. Thanks!

1. *Description of subject:* Smart dresser until recently. Has become less interested in personal appearance during the past few months. Weighs 250 pounds and is about 5' 6". Brown hair, blue eyes, and a birthmark on forehead about which Jones is very self-conscious.
2. *Criminal background:* Speeding tickets several years ago.
3. *Mental illness history:* No information. Always seemed okay.
4. *Medical history:* No information.
5. *Family background:* Large family. Some killed when Jones was young. Does not talk much about family. Mother and father live somewhere in city. Doesn't see them very much.
6. *Close relationships:* New friend. Jones and I have been friends for ten years.
7. *Significant events in the subject's life:* Recent divorce and children moving away and feeling very much alone.
8. *Activities of subject today:* No information.
9. *Information on victims or hostages:* I do not think that Jones would ever hold anybody hostage or hurt anyone.
10. *Physical description including entrances, exits, and floor plan of barricaded area or stronghold:* One-story, single-family dwelling, two bedrooms, one bath, a den, and living room. Has a gun collection and keeps lots of ammunition for target practice. Has new guns and old guns mounted on the wall of the house.

Minister of the Subject's Church

Read very carefully: This is the role that you will play in this simulation. Please use only the information provided in these instructions and in the scenario sheet. The information provided is what you will provide to the interrogators/interviewers who will talk with you at some time during the simulation. Provide *only*, I repeat *only* the information given to you. Provide this information *only* in response to specific questions about these items. This is very important. *Do not volunteer any information.* Answer questions only. **If the interviewer does not ask the specific questions to get your specific answers, make up answers to his or her questions in accordance with your understanding of the overall scenario.** The training of an interviewer is dependent on him or her knowing what questions to ask to simulation participants and your willingness to stick to your role. Under no circumstances are you to make the scenario any harder or less realistic than it is. Stick to your role at all times. Thanks!

1. *Description of subject:* Jones is a middle-age, white person who dresses nicely and always seems self-assured. Recently Jones seemed depressed and unsure of self or the future. Jones is approximately 5' 7" tall and weighs 150 pounds, but usually weighs more than does now.
2. *Criminal background:* No information.
3. *Mental illness history:* Over the past year, Jones has become more and more depressed. Jones is worried about divorce, the children, the job, and a recent diagnosis of terminal cancer. Jones said that the physical and mental pain is too much to handle.
4. *Medical history:* No information.
5. *Family background:* From a large family. Parents divorced and then remarried when Jones was small. Got along fairly well with brothers and sisters, but they were all killed in a traffic accident when Jones was eight years old. Never talks too much about it because Jones was so young at the time.
6. *Close relationships:* Seems close to the church. Has become more dependent recently. Has a friend of the opposite sex. Ex-spouse and the subject were close for many years but there is much bitterness now. The children have moved away and Jones does not know where they are. Jones depends on the job for emotional as well as financial support.
7. *Significant events in the subject's life:* Death of brothers and sisters. Divorce after many years of marriage. Current physical illness. Problems at work due to illness and the expectation of being fired.
8. *Activities of subject today:* Called church today. Minister was out and Jones left a message that Jones had called. Tried to return call to Jones but without success.
9. *Information on victims or hostages:* No information.
10. *Physical description including entrances, exits, and floor plan of barricaded area or stronghold:* No information.

Neighbor of the Subject

Read very carefully: This is the role that you will play in this simulation. Please use only the information provided in these instructions and in the scenario sheet. The information provided is what you will provide to the interrogators/interviewers who will talk with you at some time during the simulation. Provide *only*, I repeat *only* the information given to you. Provide this information *only* in response to specific questions about these items. This is very important. *Do not volunteer any information.* Answer questions only. **If the interviewer does not ask the specific questions to get your specific answers, make up answers to his or her questions in**

accordance with your understanding of the overall scenario. The training of an interviewer is dependent on him or her knowing what questions to ask to simulation participants and your willingness to stick to your role. Under no circumstances are you to make the scenario any harder or less realistic than it is. Stick to your role at all times. Thanks!

1. *Description of subject:* Nice person who is usually friendly. One hundred and sixty pounds, 5' 7", brown hair, blue eyes, with a birthmark on forehead. Usually dresses well. Lately, very messy and unkempt.

2. *Criminal background:* On the neighborhood crime watch committee. Stopped coming to meetings three to four weeks ago.

3. *Mental illness history:* No information.

4. *Medical history:* No information.

5. *Family background:* Usually kept to self and did not discuss family at all. I think that subject's mother and father live in the city. Ex-spouse may live in the city also.

6. *Close relationships:* Has had a friend who is over at the house a great deal ever since the subject moved into the house. They do not live together from all indications.

7. *Significant events in the subject's life:* No information.

8. *Activities of subject today:* Came home yesterday afternoon and did not respond when I said hello in the yard. Went directly into the house and shut the door. Later is when we heard the loud noises and shots and went to check. Would not respond when we rang the doorbell. We knocked and subject yelled at us to get away and we heard additional shots or what sounded like shots. We don't like guns and really have not been around them much.

9. *Information on victims or hostages:* Not sure if anyone is inside house with subject. Could be. Heard a lot of shouting and yelling. Could be that someone is hurt. We are not sure. We did not see anyone go into the house all day or after the subject came home. Someone could have gone in without us knowing it, however.

10. *Physical description including entrances, exits, and floor plan of barricaded area or stronghold:* One-story, brick house with two bedrooms in the back and a living room and den in the front. Front door off of living room. Back door is off of kitchen. Picture window in front. Several smaller windows in back and on the sides. Telephone in den near easy chair across from the television. Guns on the wall and other weapons. We do not know what the other weapons are.

Parents of the Subject

Read very carefully: This is the role that you will play in this simulation. Please use only the information provided in these instructions and in the scenario sheet. The information provided is what you will provide to the interrogators/interviewers who will talk with you at some time during the simulation. Provide *only,* I repeat *only* the information given to you. Provide this information *only* in response to specific questions about these items. This is very important. *Do not volunteer any information.* Answer questions only. **If the interviewer does not ask the specific questions to get your specific answers, make up answers to his or her questions in accordance with your understanding of the overall scenario.** The training of an interviewer is dependent on him or her knowing what questions to ask to simulation participants and your willingness to stick to your role. Under no circumstances are you to make the scenario any harder or less realistic than it is. Stick to your role at all times. Thanks!

1. *Description of subject:* White, forty-nine years old, 5' 7" tall, 150 pounds. Lost a lot of weight recently. Used to weigh 205. Looks drawn and haggard. Looks older than actual age.
2. *Criminal background:* No criminal history found.
3. *Mental illness history:* Has been seeing a psychiatrist.
4. *Medical history:* Recently told about being very ill with cancer. Does really not know the extent of the cancer and illness. Probably very bad. Receiving treatment.
5. *Family background:* Ex-spouse lives in city. Children have grown and moved away. Unable to contact them. Very close to children. Oldest child also terminally ill. Very little information available. Married when very young. Has a close new friend of the opposite sex now who seems to be loving and very caring. I am not sure if this person is serious about the subject or about the subject's money.
6. *Close relationships:* Close to the minister at church. Always has gone to church. Closer recently. Jones loves new friend of the opposite sex. No other friends known.
7. *Significant events in the subject's life:* Bitter divorce six months ago. Children moved away one year ago. Diagnosed as having cancer three months ago. May also have recently lost job that subject has held for many years.
8. *Activities of subject today:* No information.
9. *Information on victims or hostages:* No information.
10. *Physical description including entrances, exits, and floor plan of barricaded area or stronghold:* Single-family home with two bed-

rooms, two bathrooms, living room in the front of the house, back door, front door, attic, kitchen, den, side door.

Ex-Spouse of the Subject

Read very carefully: This is the role that you will play in this simulation. Please use only the information provided in these instructions and in the scenario sheet. The information provided is what you will provide to the interrogators/interviewers who will talk with you at some time during the simulation. Provide *only,* I repeat *only* the information given to you. Provide this information *only* in response to specific questions about these items. This is very important. *Do not volunteer any information.* Answer questions only. **If the interviewer does not ask the specific questions to get your specific answers, make up answers to his or her questions in accordance with your understanding of the overall scenario.** The training of an interviewer is dependent on him or her knowing what questions to ask to simulation participants and your willingness to stick to your role. Under no circumstances are you to make the scenario any harder or less realistic than it is. Stick to your role at all times. Thanks!

You are very angry at being disturbed by the police and really do not want to talk about your ex. The more that the interviewer asks questions, the more angry and upset you become. You finally throw the interviewer out and tell the interviewer not to come back.

1. *Description of subject:* Forty-nine years old. Subject is 5' 7" tall.
2. *Criminal background:* Several speeding tickets.
3. *Mental illness history:* Crazy person. Cannot be trusted.
4. *Medical history:* No information.
5. *Family background:* Loved children. Unfaithful to ex during marriage. Not close with parents. Has a new serious love interest.
6. *Close relationships:* Always a loner. Never asked for help from anyone.
7. *Significant events in the subject's life:* Poor self-esteem as a child. Parents divorced and remarried when subject was very young. Always upset by this.
8. *Activities of subject today:* Called yesterday to get address of children. Was not given the address.
9. *Information on victims or hostages:* No information.
10. *Physical description including entrances, exits, and floor plan of barricaded area or stronghold:* No information.

Employer of the Subject

Read very carefully: This is the role that you will play in this simulation. Please use only the information provided in these instructions and in the scenario sheet. The information provided is what you will provide to the interrogators/interviewers who will talk with you at some time during the simulation. Provide *only,* I repeat *only* the information given to you. Provide this information *only* in response to specific questions about these items. This is very important. *Do not volunteer any information.* Answer questions only. **If the interviewer does not ask the specific questions to get your specific answers, make up answers to his or her questions in accordance with your understanding of the overall scenario.** The training of an interviewer is dependent on him or her knowing what questions to ask to simulation participants and your willingness to stick to your role. Under no circumstances are you to make the scenario any harder or less realistic than it is. Stick to your role at all times. Thanks!

1. *Description of subject:* Jones is white. Subject is about fifty years old. Subject is 5' 7" tall. Jones was a good worker until recently. Seems worried and preoccupied with something serious. Attempts to ask about this have met with no response and anger.
2. *Criminal background:* Always honest at work.
3. *Mental illness history:* Always seemed okay until approximately six months ago. I think that Jones either is or was going through a bad divorce.
4. *Medical history:* Off work about one year ago with a minor foot operation. Went to doctor recently. Would not tell anybody what was wrong.
5. *Family background:* Married for twenty-five years.
6. *Close relationships:* No information.
7. *Significant events in the subject's life:* Knew that if subject's work did not improve that subject might be fired from the job. Work did not improve and Jones probably knew that I was going to have to terminate. Did not show up for work today.
8. *Activities of subject today:* No information. Called, but unable to reach the subject at home. Some of the other employees said that they had seen Jones briefly this morning.
9. *Information on victims or hostages:* No information.
10. *Physical description including entrances, exits, and floor plan of barricaded area or stronghold:* No information.

SAMPLE ROLE-PLAY EXERCISES

Please note that roles are provided for both victims and interveners. Neither victim nor intervener should see the roles of the other.

Police (PL) and Crisis Intervener/Peer Support Team Members (CI)

CI1. Husband and wife: husband is drunk.

CI2. Husband and wife: wife just came home from date with boyfriend.

CI3. Boyfriend and girlfriend: girl wants man to get divorce.

PL1. Husband and wife: husband has a weapon.

PL2. Two females in apartment: on drugs.

PL3. Two drunk males fighting over card game winnings.

CI4. Husband and wife: husband has just told wife he wants a divorce.

CI5. Two seventeen-year-old males fighting in school situation over girl-friend.

CI6. Two women (neighbors) fighting over disturbance caused by son's rock band.

PL4. Service attendant and customer fighting over repairs: attendant has a wrench.

CI7. School problem

Suicide

SU1. Despondent male at home: has a weapon in his hand, attempting suicide because wife left him.

SU2. Drunk woman with knife: despondent over loss of child, long illness.

Probation

PR1. Convicted felon is not making regular reports to probation officer, but apparently not breaking any other rules.

PR2. First-offense drug parolee is beginning to hang around with some old friends.

Developed by Ken Rensin, Louisville Division of Police, and Edward S. Rosenbluh for Crisis Training Institute.

Crisis Center

CC1. By phone, a seventeen-year-old girl calls after fight with parents over an abortion attempt; probable suicide attempt.

CC2. Attempted suicide: woman calls center after OD.

CC3. Mother and father of seventeen-year-old male comes to center as son declares he is about to leave school and home—son does *not* come to center.

Corrections

CR1. First offender (breaking and entering) begins to break minor institution rules.

CR2. Woman prisoner becomes despondent over welfare of children.

CR3. Corrections officer breaks up a fight between two prisoners over new first offender cellmate.

CI1

Wife

Your husband has come home drunk several times in the past month. He is using the household money for his drinking and this time you have called for assistance.

Husband

You have spent at least one day a week out drinking with the boys after work. Each time that you come home, your wife screams at you for spending the household money on alcohol. Your wife called for help with you this time.

Crisis Interveners/Peer Supporters (2)

You have been sent on a run to 123 Adams Street on domestic trouble. When you arrive, you can hear loud voices and the sounds of dishes breaking. The wife invites you in and it is obvious that the husband is intoxicated.

CI2

Husband

On a Friday (payday), you arrive home at the usual time. Your wife is an hour late and, when she arrives, she drives up in her boss's car. You suspect that this has happened before.

Wife

While at work, your boss asks you out for a drink after working hours. It's Friday (and payday), so you go and arrive home about an hour later than usual. Your husband is home and accuses you of running around with the boss.

Crisis Interveners/Peer Supporters (2)

You have been requested to go to 1425 Trouble Lane. As you are at the door you hear very loud voices. The husband opens the door and invites you in.

CI3

Crisis Interveners/Peer Supporters (2)

You have been asked to go to the Swinging Singles Apartment complex, apartment #10. You do not hear any apparent domestic trouble, but, when the door opens, a woman answers. She tells you she is having boyfriend trouble and he is in the apartment.

Boyfriend

You have been going with your girlfriend for some months and she has been asking you to get a divorce. To this point, you have refused and an argument starts. You are in her apartment and she calls for assistance.

Girlfriend

You have been dating a married man for some time. You have repeatedly asked him to get a divorce and he tells you, tonight, that he simply will not get a divorce. You are in your apartment and an argument follows. You have called for assistance.

PL1

Boyfriend (#2)

You have come to your new girlfriend's apartment. As the two of you are on the sofa having a drink and watching television, there is a knock at the door. Another man comes in and, as soon as he sees you, he draws a gun and threatens to shoot you.

Police Officers (2)

You have a trouble run to 2345 Nasty Lane. On arrival, you hear loud voices and, as the woman opens the door, you see a man on one side of the room behind a chair and another on the other side of the room pointing a gun.

Boyfriend (#1)

You have come to settle with your girlfriend. As she opens the door, she is on the sofa with another man. Suspecting that this has happened before, you pull a loaded weapon and threaten to shoot the other man.

Girlfriend

You have invited a new boyfriend over to your home. While he is there, your other boyfriend knocks. When you answer the door, he comes in and sees the other man. He draws a gun and starts to yell. You call the police.

PL2

Police Officers (2)

On a trouble run to 123 Mary Jane Street, you knock at the door and it is opened by a woman. She invites you in and you notice that the air has a heavy, sweet odor; in addition, several chairs are knocked over and there are broken dishes on the floor.

Girl #1

You have invited your next-door neighbor into your apartment for a drink. During the evening, she offers you some marijuana cigarettes. You are both smoking when your friend starts to complain about the loud music you had on last night. The argument continues, with your friend knocking over some chairs and becoming very loud. There is a knock at the door.

Girl #2

Your neighbor invites you to her apartment for a drink. During the evening you offer her some marijuana cigarettes that you got from a friend. During the past few evenings, your neighbor has been playing the television set very loud. You mention this and she gets upset. The argument gets louder and you knock over the dining room chair. There is a knock at the door.

PL3

Police Officers (2)

Radio has sent you on a trouble run to the Hangout Saloon. The bartender says that two men in the back room have been having an argument.

Man #1

You and your fellow employee have gone to the Hangout Saloon for a few beers after work. You decide to have a small poker game and, during the game, you feel your friend is cheating. You tell him you want a new deck of cards or you will leave. Your friend gets upset and an argument follows.

Man #2

You and a fellow employee have gone to the Hangout Saloon for a few beers after work. You have a small poker game and midway through the game, your friend insists on having a new deck of cards or he will leave. You feel he is accusing you of cheating and an argument follows.

CI4

Crisis Interveners/Peer Supports (2)

On a domestic trouble request for assistance, you arrive at 9675 Divorce Lane and find an argument in progress. The husband invites you into the home.

Husband

You have been having trouble with your wife for some time. You have hinted that you would like a divorce, but tonight, after dinner, you come out and tell her that you want a divorce. A violent argument follows and you call for assistance.

Wife

After dinner your husband comes out and tells you that he wants a divorce. You have not seen any sign of this in the past and you become very upset. A violent argument follows and your husband calls for assistance.

CI5

Student #1

You and another friend get in a fight in the rear of the school over your girlfriend. He has a small caliber pistol with him. You both are seniors.

Student #2

You and another senior have a fight in the rear of the school over your friend's girl. You are dating her now and he is getting in the way. Because you thought a fight might occur, you have taken your father's 22 caliber pistol to school with you.

Crisis Interveners/Peer Supporters (2)

You are called by a colleague to go to a local high school. On arrival the principal tells you that the two seniors have been fighting out back; one may have a weapon.

CI6

Woman #1

Your neighbor's son has a rock band that always rehearses in her garage. It is 11:00 p.m. and they are still playing. You call for help and go out on the front lawn. The boy's mother comes out on the porch and an argument starts on the lawn.

Woman #2

Your son has a rock band that rehearses in your garage. It is now 11:00 p.m. and the band is still there. You walk out on the porch and see your neighbor (female) on the front lawn. An argument starts on the lawn.

Crisis Interveners/Peer Supporters (2)

You have a "neighbor trouble run" and, on arrival, both women are screaming on the front lawn. There is loud music in the background and both women appear to be older.

PL4

Police Officers (2)

You have a run to the local garage. When you arrive, you see the owner, with a wrench in his hands, arguing with a customer. There is a car in the shop with the hood up.

Garage Owner

You have worked all day on tuning a customer's car. When he arrives, he is not satisfied with the work and states that you overcharged him. He pushes you away and you pick up a wrench.

Customer

You have had a tune-up at the local garage. When you arrive, the hood is still up and the motor does not sound right. The owner hands you the bill and you feel it is way overpriced. An argument starts and you shove the owner. He reaches for a wrench.

SU1

Husband

Your wife told you this afternoon that she is leaving you. After a long argument, you get a revolver and chase your wife out of the house. Your three-year-old child is still at home. You have stated before that suicide may be the only way out.

Crisis Interveners/Peer Supporters (2)

You have received a "man with a gun" run. At the scene you are met by the wife and she states that her husband is down the block (at home) with one of the children (age three) and has a gun. She has stated he will kill himself and the child.

SU2

Crisis Interveners/Peer Supporters (2)

You have a "woman with a knife" run at a local apartment. On your arrival, a woman is sitting at a table with a knife and a drink on the table.

Woman

You have just had a twelve-year-old son die after a bout with cancer. It is the second time one of your children has died and you start heavy drinking. In your pocket, you have a knife your son made in school and you leave it on the table.

PR1

Parole Officer

You have a convicted felon (auto theft—first offense) apparently breaking some minor rules. So far he has not been in any trouble.

Parolee

You are a twenty-one-year-old first offender (auto theft) on probation. You find the "small" rules (home on time, don't drive, etc.) rather silly. You have broken some of the rules, but have done nothing serious, yet.

PR2

Parole Officer

You have a twenty-year-old first offender (drugs) that is starting to hang around with some of his old friends.

Parolee

As a first offender, twenty-year-old male (drug charge), you have been seeing some of the "old gang" the past few weeks. Your parole officer calls you to his office.

CC1

Crisis Center Worker

While on duty at the center, a call comes in *by phone.* When you answer, you have a female voice on the other end that is rambling on about her parents and a baby. The tone is slow, low, and stumbling.

Female

You are a seventeen-year-old female who just had a violent argument with your parents about an abortion attempt. You are five months pregnant and you have just taken some sleeping pills, but before finishing the bottle you *call* the crisis center.

CC2

Crisis Center Worker

By phone, you receive a call from an older female stating that she has just taken an overdose of sleeping pills.

Female

You are a forty-year-old woman. Your husband has just walked out on you. You have taken a full bottle of sleeping pills, but before passing out you *call* the crisis center.

CC3

Crisis Center Worker

Two parents come to the center. They are having a large problem with their seventeen-year-old son. The boy refused to come to the center.

Father and Mother

You are the parents of a seventeen-year-old son. Last night, he came home at 3 a.m. and has stated repeatedly that he is quitting school (senior year) and is leaving home. Your son refuses to come to the center.

CR1

Corrections Officer

You have just noticed a first offender (twenty-one years old), who is about to break some of the minor institution rules. To date, he has been in no serious trouble. He was convicted of breaking and entering.

Prisoner

You are a first offender, twenty-one years old, and in prison for breaking and entering. You find some of the small prison rules (smoking, talking in line, etc.) childish. You have not been in any serious trouble while confined.

CR2

Corrections Officer

It has been called to your attention that a first-offender female inmate is becoming despondent. Your "grapevine" information is that she may attempt suicide.

Prisoner

You are a twenty-two-year-old female prisoner (first offense) and have two children. Your husband has left you and your mother came last visiting day and told you she could no longer care for your children. The only recourse is a state home. You have considered suicide before, while awaiting trial.

CR3

Prisoner #1

You are a lifer (armed robbery) and have just been in a fight with another prisoner (lifer) who you thought was leading a new first offender into possible homosexual circumstances. During the fight, you have been cut by the other inmate.

Corrections Officer

You have just broken up a fight between two "lifers" over an apparent quarrel over a new (male) inmate. One of the disputes has a reputation as a homosexual. One prisoner has been cut on the arm.

Prisoner #2

You are a "lifer" (manslaughter) and you have just been in a fight with another inmate. You have a prison reputation as a possible homosexual and the argument started with the other prisoner because he thought you were trying to persuade another first offender to go back to your cell.

CI7

Counselor

As a counselor at a high school, several teachers report that one sixteen-year-old junior is failing all her courses and is becoming a discipline problem in all of her classes. Your records reflect a very high IQ and good grammar school marks.

Girl

You are a sixteen-year-old high-school junior. You were always at the top of your class, but, during the last year, you have slacked off on your studies. As your grades dropped, both parents and teachers kept saying how good you "used" to be in school and your father has told you if your grades do not improve he will take away all your social activities. Right now, you are failing all your courses and finding school a "drag."

Appendix III

The Hostage and Crisis Negotiator's Training Lab

This chapter describes the development of a hostage negotiations training laboratory (HNTL) designed as a state-of-the-art learning center, and to be used as a vital part of the current basic, intermediate, advanced and in-service training that negotiators now receive. Such a laboratory provides multiple opportunities for negotiator trainees, at their various levels of expertise, to practice basic communications and negotiations skills learned in class. This is accomplished under the guidance and supervision of the class instructor, laboratory director, and other experienced negotiators.

Students are able to work, either as a member of a team or individually, on preprogrammed hostage and barricade crisis scenarios that have been developed based on actual situations occurring in the field. They are given basic information on a specific scenario that allows them to initiate contact and begin negotiations with actual role players representing themselves as hostage takers or barricaded subjects. Over a preprogrammed period of time, each student is given additional information that tests their abilities to analyze and to integrate such information into their negotiations strategy. Each student is rated according to a "specific skill"-type rating sheet. Ratings are done by the course instructor or laboratory director, the role-players, and student raters.

At the end of the preprogrammed time period allotted for each scenario presented, each student negotiator is debriefed and given feedback based on his or her performance and score on the rating sheet. Such information is stored for future use as a comparison between current and past performance and improvement therein.

STATEMENT OF THE PROBLEM

The growing complexity of police work in general and of dealing with crisis scenarios, such as hostage, barricaded, and suicidal situations specifically, dictates the need for highly specialized training and training modalities that will better equip the police crisis negotiator. The intricacies of human relationships and of interpersonal communications are at the foundation of successful negotiations in these situations. Development of skills in these areas are discussed in classroom settings where negotiators are trained. Role-playing is often used to assist the negotiator in perfecting the needed skills. This may not be enough.

HISTORY AND BACKGROUND INFORMATION

Proper and accepted current thinking about the handling of hostage, barricaded, and suicidal incidents indicates that those police personnel who are best trained in hostage negotiations procedures have the best chance of bringing about a successful resolution to a given incident.

Success in these situations is usually defined as a resolution in which there is no loss of life to any of those involved in the incident including police, hostage taker, and hostages.

Tactical team involvement is a must so that proper containment of the situation can be accomplished. With this containment, negotiations techniques are maximally effective.

In hostage situations, when properly trained negotiators are allowed to do the job for which they were trained, and are given the required amount of time necessary, and are given the support that they need, the incidence of death to the hostages, hostage taker, or to anyone else involved is drastically reduced.

DESIGN

The hostage negotiations training laboratory is set up in a standard classroom (see Figure A3.1). Student negotiators are separated from the role-players by study carrels or room dividers. Each individual student or team of students has their own designated carrel or enclosure that reduces the distractions of other student teams. Contact with the hostage taker/role-player (HTRP) is by telephone in most cases. The lab is arranged so that some negotiations can be done in a semi–face-to-face mode as needed. Each student negotiator (SN) is given a scenario sheet that gives only the basic facts of the situation which he/she is about to encounter. After a brief period that is used to review this information, the SN makes contact by telephone with the HTRP and begins negotiations. The HTRP is thoroughly briefed and scripted for each scenario undertaken and will be monitored throughout by the course instructor or laboratory director. Strict guidelines for the HTRP are

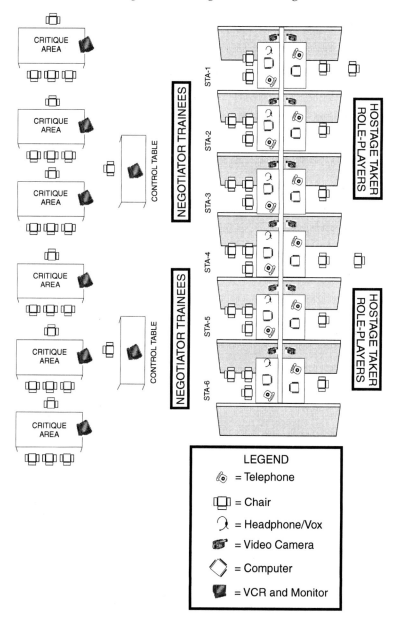

FIGURE A3.1. Detailed Diagram of Proposed Hostage and Crisis Negotiations Training Laboratory

employed. Figure A3.2 is a close-up diagram of the individual modules, equipment, and critique area of the hostage and crisis negotiations training laboratory. Figure A3.3 is a close-up of the hostage negotiations training laboratory modules and control area.

Ratings

Each SN is rated on a score sheet specifically developed for the scenario undertaken. Ratings are done by a member or the SN's team or by a student rater in the case of individual utilization of the lab. Similar ratings are done by the HTRP and by the course instructor, the laboratory director, or his supervised agent or assistant instructor. Rating sheet scores are based on a point system with points given for utilization of specific negotiations and crisis intervention skills appropriate to the specific scenario. Points are not subtracted for nonutilization of skills but are given if a necessary skill is demonstrated. Minimum score levels are needed to successfully complete the scenario when this laboratory exercise is used as part of overall negotiator proficiency testing.

Additional Input to the Scenario

During the predetermined time for the specific scenario, additional information is given to the SN by the instructor as would be the case in an actual situation when intelligence information is being gathered. Integration of this information into the negotiations plan of the SN also is scored by the raters. The scenario is automatically terminated at the end of the predetermined time period.

Debriefing of Student Negotiators

Immediately, subsequent to the termination of the scenario and the completion and collection of all rating sheets, the SN is debriefed in a separate and insulated area of the laboratory. The rating sheets are utilized to discuss, and to allow for both self and other evaluation of, the SN's performance. These ratings are stored for retrieval during future laboratory exercises for comparison of student performance and improvement. Debriefings are conducted by the student rater, the SN's team rater, the course instructors, and the laboratory director, as appropriate. Self-evaluation and development of action plans for improvement of skills are emphasized.

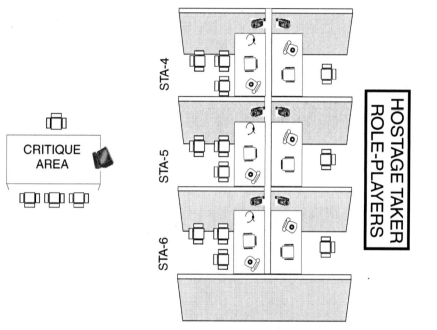

FIGURE A3.2. Close-Up Diagram of HNTL Individual Modules, Equipment, and Critique Area

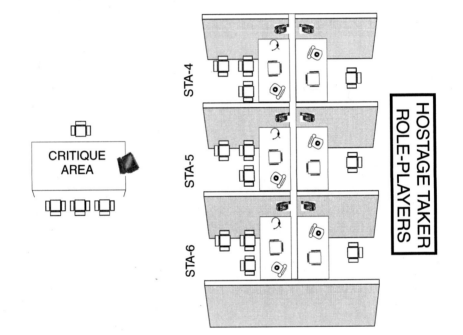

FIGURE A3.3. Close-Up Diagram of HNTL Modules and Control Area

Additional Programs to Be Utilized in the HNTL

The additional training modalities mentioned earlier in this proposal include:

1. Programs allowing the SN to analyze and evaluate specific critical incidents and to receive feedback on their performance
2. Communication exercises
3. Specialized negotiations techniques
4. Specialized crisis-intervention modalities
5. Diagnostic skill training

The laboratory also can be used for police training in the areas of:

6. Investigations and interrogations
7. Interpersonal relations
8. Abuse situations
9. Media relations
10. Basic crisis intervention skills

Product

It is often the case that both in classroom training as well as in more elaborate simulations of hostage, barricaded, and crisis situations, not all students may be able to acquire as much negotiations practice time as they may need to sharpen various negotiations and negotiations-related skills. Therefore, it is anticipated that, based on the equipment available and utilized, multiple students can participate in the same or different scenarios simultaneously (see Figure A3.1). In addition, the specific skills on which they may need to work can be anticipated and needed training enhanced in this laboratory setting. The laboratory is designed so that a student can utilize the laboratory individually or as a member of a student team. Each may be done depending on the specific needs and intent of the student and the recommendations of the instructor or the laboratory director.

The laboratory can be expanded to meet the needs of large numbers of students and such expansion depends primarily on the availability of needed equipment as indicated. Skill-development needs discovered in the classroom or during simulations can be examined in the laboratory and addressed specifically. Skills that are enhanced by laboratory training will find outlets during the didactic and practical aspects of the negotiations or crisis management course to the obvious benefit of the student negotiator.

In addition to the preprogrammed telephone for face-to-face negotiations experiences, scenarios have also been developed that allow the SN to analyze and evaluate hostage scenes, specific negotiations problems, crisis situations, "do's and don't's," diagnostic criteria, and other related problems. Feedback can be computerized so that a student may work at a personally appropriate speed to assure maximum learning.

Communication exercises are also available for the SN to utilize as needed with appropriate feedback and illustrations.

Specialized negotiations techniques, which have been sufficiently covered in class, are available in the laboratory also. SNs can review these methods and practice their utilization in a controlled environment and to the extent necessary to assure maximum comprehension and application.

Facilities Needed

Basically, a large room within which carrels, telephone equipment, computers, video equipment, tables, and chairs can be replaced. This room should also be available twenty-four hours per day, have outside access, and be able to be secured independently.

Equipment Needed

> Room dividers
> Carrels/multiple stations
> Phone systems
> Video cameras/monitoring and recording
> Audio monitoring and recording
> Computers for tracking ratings and data entry and storage
> Debriefing carrels
> Research assistance—data entry and evaluation
> Tracking devices for each student
> Audio and video equipment for student feedback and debriefing after negotiations
> Rating sheets
> Miscellaneous supplies
> Copy facilities
> Semipermanent storage of all negotiations in laboratory
> Scenario programs
> Miscellaneous electronic equipment and spare parts

Test Hostage Negotiations Training Laboratories

The prototype for the hostage negotiations training laboratory was developed by Dr. James Greenstone. It was originally utilized at the North Central Texas Council of Governments Regional Police Academy in basic, advanced, and accelerated hostage negotiations training programs.

Videotaping and Audiotaping of Laboratories

Performance in the laboratory setting is videotaped and the negotiations are audiotaped for review by the SN and the course instructor. They are maintained for future review and comparisons of performance.

Monitoring of Laboratory Negotiations

All negotiations undertaken by SNs in the HNTL are monitored by the course or the laboratory director. Such monitoring can be undertaken either personally or by electronic means.

It is anticipated that this laboratory setting will be used to enhance the negotiations skills of law enforcement officers working in this important area.

Appendix IV

Additional Reference Materials

THE BILL OF RIGHTS

Amendment I

Congress shall make no law respecting an establishment of religion, or prohibiting the free exercise thereof; or abridging the freedom of speech, or of the press; or the right of the people peaceably to assemble, and to petition the Government for a redress of grievances.

Amendment II

A well regulated Militia, being necessary to the security of a free State, the right of the people to keep and bear Arms, shall not be infringed.

Amendment III

No Soldier shall, in time of peace be quartered in any house, without the consent of the Owner, nor in time of war, but in a manner to be prescribed by law.

Amendment IV

The right of the people to be secure in their persons, houses, papers, and effects, against unreasonable searches and seizures, shall not be violated, and no Warrants shall issue, but upon probable cause, supported by Oath or affirmation, and particularly describing the place to be searched, and the persons or things to be seized.

Amendment V

No person shall be held to answer for a capital, or otherwise infamous crime, unless on a presentment or indictment of a Grand Jury, except in cases arising in the land or naval forces, or in the Militia, when in actual service in time of War or public danger; nor shall any person be subject for the same offence to be twice put in jeopardy of life or limb; nor shall be compelled in any criminal case to be a witness against himself, nor be deprived of life, liberty, or property, without due process of law; nor shall private property be taken for public use, without just compensation.

Amendment VI

In all criminal prosecutions, the accused shall enjoy the right to a speedy and public trial, by an impartial jury of the State and district wherein the crime shall have been committed, which district shall have been previously ascertained by law, and to be informed of the nature and cause of the accusation; to be confronted with the witnesses against him; to have compulsory process for obtaining witnesses in his favor, and to have the Assistance of Counsel for his defence.

Amendment VII

In Suits at common law, where the value in controversy shall exceed twenty dollars, the right of trial by jury shall be preserved, and no fact tried by a jury, shall be otherwise reexamined in any Court of the United States, than according to the rules of the common law.

Amendment VIII

Excessive bail shall not be required, nor excessive fines imposed, nor cruel and unusual punishments inflicted.

Amendment IX

The enumeration in the Constitution, of certain rights, shall not be construed to deny or disparage others retained by the people.

Amendment X

The powers not delegated to the United States by the Constitution, nor prohibited by it to the States, are reserved to the States respectively, or to the people.

OVERVIEW OF THE U.S. CONSTITUTION

Only a very basic overview is provided here to acquaint the reader with the provisions of the U.S. Constitution. For additional information, refer to the complete document.

Preamble

We the People of the United States, in Order to form a more perfect Union, establish Justice, insure domestic Tranquility, provide for the common defense, promote the general Welfare, and secure the Blessings of Liberty to ourselves and our Posterity, do ordain and establish this Constitution for the United States of America.

Article I: The Legislative Branch

Section 1. "All legislative Powers herein granted . . ."
Section 2. "The House of Representatives shall be composed . . ."
Section 3. "The Senate of the United States shall be composed . . ."
Section 4. "The Times, Places and Manner of holding Elections . . ."
Section 5. "Each House shall be the Judge . . ."
Section 6. "The Senators and Representatives shall receive a Compensation . . ."
Section 7. "All Bills for raising Revenue shall originate . . ."
Section 8. "The Congress shall have Power To lay and collect Taxes . . ."
Section 9. "The Migration or Importation of such Persons . . ."
Section 10. "No State shall enter into any Treaty . . ."

Article II: The Executive Branch

Section 1. "The executive Power shall be vested in a President . . ."
Section 2. "The President shall be Commander in Chief . . ."
Section 3. "He shall from time to time give to the Congress Information . . ."
Section 4. "The President, Vice President and all civil Officers of the United States . . ."

Article III: The Judicial Branch

Section 1. "The judicial Power of the United States . . ."
Section 2. "The judicial Power shall extend to all Cases . . ."
Section 3. "Treason against the United States . . ."

Article IV: Relations Between the States

Section 1. "Full Faith and Credit shall be given . . ."
Section 2. "The Citizens of each State shall be entitled to all Privileges and Immunities . . ."
Section 3. "New States may be admitted by the Congress . . ."
Section 4. "The United States shall guarantee to every State . . ."

Article V: The Amendment Process

Article VI: General Provisions, Supremacy of the Constitution

Article VII: Ratification Process

TEXAS PENAL CODE

These are sections of Texas law that pertain in some way to hostage taking and hostage negotiations. Laws will vary on these subjects from state to state. Negotiators should know the relevant laws in their jurisdiction. These are provided as illustrative examples only.

§ 20.04. Aggravated Kidnapping

(a) A person commits an offense if he intentionally or knowingly abducts another person with the intent to:
    (1) hold him for ransom or reward;
    (2) use him as a shield or hostage;
    (3) facilitate the commission of a felony or the flight after the attempt or commission of a felony;
    (4) inflict bodily injury on him or violate or abuse him sexually;
    (5) terrorize him or a third person; or
    (6) interfere with the performance of any governmental or political function.
(b) A person commits an offense if the person intentionally or knowingly abducts another person and uses or exhibits a deadly weapon during the commission of the offense.
(c) Except as provided by Subsection (d), an offense under this section is a felony of the first degree.
(d) At the punishment stage of a trial, the defendant may raise the issue as to whether he voluntarily released the victim in a safe place. If the defendant proves the issue in the affirmative by a preponderance of the evidence, the offense is a felony of the second degree.

Acts 1973, 63rd Leg., p. 883, ch. 399, § 1, eff. Jan. 1, 1974. Amended by Acts 1993, 73rd Leg., ch. 900, § 1.01, eff. Sept. 1, 1994.

Amended by Acts 1995, 74th Leg., ch. 318, § 4, eff. Sept. 1, 1995.

§ 16.02. Unlawful Interception, Use, or Disclosure of Wire, Oral, or Electronic Communications

Text of section effective until Sept. 1, 2005

(a) In this section, "covert entry," "communication common carrier," "contents," "electronic, mechanical, or other device," "intercept," "investigative or law enforcement officer," "oral communication," "electronic communication," "readily accessible to the general public," and "wire communication" have the meanings given those terms in Article 18.20, Code of Criminal Procedure.

(b) A person commits an offense if he:

    (1) intentionally intercepts, endeavors to intercept, or procures another person to intercept or endeavor to intercept a wire, oral, or electronic communication;

    (2) intentionally discloses or endeavors to disclose to another person the contents of a wire, oral, or electronic communication if he knows or has reason to know the information was obtained through the interception of a wire, oral, or electronic communication in violation of this subsection;

    (3) intentionally uses or endeavors to use the contents of a wire, oral, or electronic communication if the person knows or is reckless about whether the information was obtained through the interception of a wire, oral, or electronic communication in violation of this subsection;

    (4) knowingly or intentionally effects a covert entry for the purpose of intercepting wire, oral, or electronic communications without court order or authorization; or

    (5) intentionally uses, endeavors to use, or procures any other person to use or endeavor to use any electronic, mechanical, or other device to intercept any oral communication when the device:

        (A) is affixed to, or otherwise transmits a signal through a wire, cable, or other connection used in wire communications; or

        (B) transmits communications by radio or interferes with the transmission of communications by radio.

(c) It is an affirmative defense to prosecution under Subsection (b) that:

    (1) an operator of a switchboard or an officer, employee, or agent of a communication common carrier whose facilities are used in the transmission of a wire or electronic communication intercepts a

communication or discloses or uses an intercepted communication in the normal course of employment while engaged in an activity that is a necessary incident to the rendition of service or to the protection of the rights or property of the carrier of the communication, unless the interception results from the communication common carrier's use of service observing or random monitoring for purposes other than mechanical or service quality control checks;

(2) an officer, employee, or agent of a communication common carrier provides information, facilities, or technical assistance to an investigative or law enforcement officer who is authorized as provided by this article to intercept a wire, oral, or electronic communication;

(3) a person acting under color of law intercepts a wire, oral, or electronic communication if the person is a party to the communication or if one of the parties to the communication has given prior consent to the interception;

(4) a person not acting under color of law intercepts a wire, oral, or electronic communication if the person is a party to the communication or if one of the parties to the communication has given prior consent to the interception unless the communication is intercepted for the purpose of committing any criminal or tortious act in violation of the constitution or laws of the United States or of this state or for the purpose of committing any other injurious act;

(5) a person acting under color of law intercepts a wire, oral, or electronic communication if:
   (A) oral or written consent for the interception is given by a magistrate before the interception;
   (B) an immediate life-threatening situation exists;
   (C) the person is a member of a law enforcement unit specially trained to:
      (i) respond to and deal with life-threatening situations; or
      (ii) install electronic, mechanical, or other devices; and
   (D) the interception ceases immediately on termination of the life-threatening situation;

(6) an officer, employee, or agent of the Federal Communications Commission intercepts a communication transmitted by radio or discloses or uses an intercepted communication in the normal course of employment and in the discharge of the monitoring responsibilities exercised by the Federal Communications Commission in the enforcement of Chapter 5, Title 47, United States Code;

(7) a person intercepts or obtains access to an electronic communication that was made through an electronic communication system

that is configured to permit the communication to be readily accessible to the general public;

(8) a person intercepts radio communication, other than a cordless telephone communication that is transmitted between a cordless telephone handset and a base unit, that is transmitted:

(A) by a station for the use of the general public;

(B) to ships, aircraft, vehicles, or persons in distress;

(C) by a governmental, law enforcement, civil defense, private land mobile, or public safety communications system that is readily accessible to the general public, unless the radio communication is transmitted by a law enforcement representative to or from a mobile data terminal;

(D) by a station operating on an authorized frequency within the bands allocated to the amateur, citizens band, or general mobile radio services; or

(E) by a marine or aeronautical communications system;

(9) a person intercepts a wire or electronic communication the transmission of which causes harmful interference to a lawfully operating station or consumer electronic equipment, to the extent necessary to identify the source of the interference;

(10) a user of the same frequency intercepts a radio communication made through a system that uses frequencies monitored by individuals engaged in the provision or the use of the system, if the communication is not scrambled or encrypted; or

(11) a provider of electronic communications service records the fact that a wire or electronic communication was initiated or completed in order to protect the provider, another provider furnishing service toward the completion of the communication, or a user of that service from fraudulent, unlawful, or abusive use of the service.

(d) A person commits an offense if he:

(1) intentionally manufactures, assembles, possesses, or sells an electronic, mechanical, or other device knowing or having reason to know that the device is designed primarily for nonconsensual interception of wire, electronic, or oral communications and that the device or a component of the device has been or will be used for an unlawful purpose; or

(2) places in a newspaper, magazine, handbill, or other publication an advertisement of an electronic, mechanical, or other device:

(A) knowing or having reason to know that the device is designed primarily for nonconsensual interception of wire, electronic, or oral communications;

> > (B) promoting the use of the device for the purpose of non-consensual interception of wire, electronic, or oral communications; or
> > (C) knowing or having reason to know that the advertisement will promote the use of the device for the purpose of nonconsensual interception of wire, electronic, or oral communications.

(e) It is an affirmative defense to prosecution under Subsection (d) that the manufacture, assembly, possession, or sale of an electronic, mechanical, or other device that is designed primarily for the purpose of non-consensual interception of wire, electronic, or oral communication is by:

> (1) a communication common carrier or a provider of wire or electronic communications service or an officer, agent, or employee of or a person under contract with a communication common carrier or provider acting in the normal course of the provider's or communication carrier's business;
> (2) an officer, agent, or employee of a person under contract with, bidding on contracts with, or doing business with the United States or this state acting in the normal course of the activities of the United States or this state; or
> (3) a law enforcement agency that has an established unit specifically designated to respond to and deal with life-threatening situations or specifically trained to install wire, oral, or electronic communications intercept equipment.

(f) Except as provided by Subsections (d) and (h), an offense under this section is a felony of the second degree.

(g) For purposes of this section:

> (1) An immediate life-threatening situation exists when human life is directly threatened in either a hostage or barricade situation.
> (2) "Member of a law enforcement unit specially trained to respond to and deal with life-threatening situations" means a peace officer who has received a minimum of 40 hours a year of training in hostage and barricade suspect situations. This training must be evidenced by the submission of appropriate documentation to the Commission on Law Enforcement Officer Standards and Education.

(h) (1) A person commits an offense if, knowing that a government attorney or an investigative or law enforcement officer has been authorized or has applied for authorization to intercept wire, electronic, or oral communications, the person obstructs, impedes, prevents, gives notice to another of, or attempts to give notice to another of the interception.

(2) An offense under this subsection is a state jail felony.

(i) This section expires September 1, 2005, and shall not be in force on and after that date.

Added by Acts 1981, 67th Leg., p. 738, ch. 275, § 2, eff. Aug. 31, 1981. Amended by Acts 1983, 68th Leg., p. 4878, ch. 864, §§ 1 to 3, eff. June 19, 1983; Acts 1989, 71st Leg., ch. 1166, § 16, eff. Sept. 1, 1989; Acts 1993, 73rd Leg., ch. 790, § 16, eff. Sept. 1, 1993; Acts 1993, 73rd Leg., ch. 900, § 1.01, eff. Sept. 1, 1994.

Amended by Acts 1997, 75th Leg., ch. 1051, § 9, eff. Sept. 1, 1997; Acts 2001, 77th Leg., ch. 1270, § 11, eff. Sept. 1, 2001.

TEXAS CODE OF CRIMINAL PROCEDURE

Art. 18.20. Interception and Use of Wire, Oral, or Electronic Communications

Text of article effective until September 1, 2005

Definitions

Sec. 1. In this article:
(1) "Wire communication" means an aural transfer made in whole or in part through the use of facilities for the transmission of communications by the aid of wire, cable, or other like connection between the point of origin and the point of reception, including the use of such a connection in a switching station, furnished or operated by a person authorized to engage in providing or operating the facilities for the transmission of communications as a communications common carrier. The term includes the electronic storage of a wire communication.
(2) "Oral communication" means an oral communication uttered by a person exhibiting an expectation that the communication is not subject to interception under circumstances justifying that expectation. The term does not include an electronic communication.
(3) "Intercept" means the aural or other acquisition of the contents of a wire, oral, or electronic communication through the use of an electronic, mechanical, or other device.
(4) "Electronic, mechanical, or other device" means a device that may be used for the nonconsensual interception of wire, oral, or electronic communications. The term does not include a telephone or telegraph instrument, the equipment or a facility used for the transmission of electronic communications, or a component of the equipment or a facility used for the transmission of electronic

communications if the instrument, equipment, facility, or component is:

    (A) furnished to the subscriber or user by a provider of wire or electronic communications service in the ordinary course of the provider's business and being used by the subscriber or user in the ordinary course of its business;

    (B) furnished by a subscriber or user for connection to the facilities of a wire or electronic communications service for use in the ordinary course of the subscriber's or user's business;

    (C) being used by a communications common carrier in the ordinary course of its business; or

    (D) being used by an investigative or law enforcement officer in the ordinary course of the officer's duties.

(5) "Investigative or law enforcement officer" means an officer of this state or of a political subdivision of this state who is empowered by law to conduct investigations of or to make arrests for offenses enumerated in Section 4 of this article or an attorney authorized by law to prosecute or participate in the prosecution of the enumerated offenses.

(6) "Contents," when used with respect to a wire, oral, or electronic communication, includes any information concerning the substance, purport, or meaning of that communication.

(7) "Judge of competent jurisdiction" means a judge from the panel of nine active district judges with criminal jurisdiction appointed by the presiding judge of the court of criminal appeals as provided by Section 3 of this article.

(8) "Prosecutor" means a district attorney, criminal district attorney, or county attorney performing the duties of a district attorney, with jurisdiction in the county within an administrative judicial district described by Section 3(b).

(9) "Director" means the director of the Department of Public Safety or, if the director is absent or unable to serve, the assistant director of the Department of Public Safety.

(10) "Communication common carrier" means a person engaged as a common carrier for hire in the transmission of wire or electronic communications.

(11) "Aggrieved person" means a person who was a party to an intercepted wire, oral, or electronic communication or a person against whom the interception was directed.

(12) "Covert entry" means any entry into or onto premises which if made without a court order allowing such an entry under this Act, would be a violation of the Penal Code.

(13) "Residence" means a structure or the portion of a structure used as a person's home or fixed place of habitation to which the person indicates an intent to return after any temporary absence.

(14) "Pen register" means a device that attaches to a telephone line and records or decodes electronic or other impulses to identify numbers dialed or otherwise transmitted on the telephone line. The term does not include a device used by a provider or customer of:

    (A) a wire or electronic communication service for purposes of charging a fee for the service; or

    (B) a wire communication service during the ordinary course of the provider's or customer's business, including cost accounting and security control.

(15) "Electronic communication" means a transfer of signs, signals, writing, images, sounds, data, or intelligence of any nature transmitted in whole or in part by a wire, radio, electromagnetic, photoelectronic, or photo-optical system. The term does not include:

    (A) a wire or oral communication;

    (B) a communication made through a tone-only paging device; or

    (C) a communication from a tracking device.

(16) "User" means a person who uses an electronic communications service and is authorized by the provider of the service to use the service.

(17) "Electronic communications system" means a wire, radio, electromagnetic, photo-optical or photoelectronic facility for the transmission of wire or electronic communications, and any computer facility or related electronic equipment for the electronic storage of those communications.

(18) "Electronic communications service" means a service that provides to users of the service the ability to send or receive wire or electronic communications.

(19) "Readily accessible to the general public" means, with respect to a radio communication, a communication that is not:

    (A) scrambled or encrypted;

    (B) transmitted using modulation techniques whose essential parameters have been withheld from the public with the intention of preserving the privacy of the communication;

    (C) carried on a subcarrier or other signal subsidiary to a radio transmission;

    (D) transmitted over a communication system provided by a common carrier, unless the communication is a tone-only paging system communication;

    (E) transmitted on frequencies allocated under Part 25, Subpart D, E, or F of Part 74, or Part 94 of the rules of the Federal

Communications Commission, unless, in the case of a communication transmitted on a frequency allocated under Part 74 that is not exclusively allocated to broadcast auxiliary services, the communication is a two-way voice communication by radio; or

(F) an electronic communication.

(20) "Electronic storage" means:

(A) a temporary, intermediate storage of a wire or electronic communication that is incidental to the electronic transmission of the communication; or

(B) storage of a wire or electronic communication by an electronic communications service for purposes of backup protection of the communication.

(21) "Aural transfer" means a transfer containing the human voice at any point between and including the point of origin and the point of reception.

(22) "Immediate life-threatening situation" means a hostage, barricade, or similar emergency situation in which human life is directly threatened.

(23) "Member of a law enforcement unit specially trained to respond to and deal with life-threatening situations" means a peace officer who receives a minimum of 40 hours a year of training in hostage and barricade suspect situations as evidenced by the submission of appropriate documentation to the Commission on Law Enforcement Officer Standards and Education.

See also the Federal Wire Tap Laws and the Federal Kidnapping Laws for additional information.

Order to Consent to Interception of Wire and Oral Communication Sample Pleadings

EX PARTE	)	No
STATE OF TEXAS	)	
	)	IN THE COURT OF
	)	TARRANT COUNTY,
	)	TEXAS
	)	
	)	
	)	
	)	
	)	
	)	

ORDER
IN RE: CONSENT TO INTERCEPT WIRE OR
ORAL COMMUNICATIONS PURSUANT TO SECTION 16.02(C)(5)
OF THE TEXAS PENAL CODE

I, _____ Judge of the_____Court of Tarrant County, Texas, on the _____ day of_____, _____ at _____o'clock_____.m, did personally talk with _____ of the Fort Worth Police Department. This conversation was conducted over the telephone and was recorded. In this conversation, _____ stated the following:

1. He or she is a member of a law enforcement unit specially trained to respond to and deal with life-threatening situations, as stated in Section 16.02(i)(2);
2. That he or she and other members of his or her unit had responded to a life-threatening situation at _____, Tarrant County, Texas, where an individual, or individuals was/were holding one or more hostages, and/or was barricaded inside of the aforesaid location.
3. The identit(y)(ies) of the hostage taker(s) or barricaded suspect(s) and his or her description(s) is/are:
4. The identit(y)(ies) of the hostage(s) and his or her or their descriptions is/are:
5. The suspect(s) has/have committed the following offenses:
6. That the suspect(s) are believed armed with the following weapons/ or is/are making the following threats:
7. That the state of mind of the suspect(s) is believed to be:
8. The state of mind of the hostage(s) is believed to be:
9. That the building, house, enclosure, or other location of the life-threatening situation is described as:
10. That this situation, based upon information gathered by: _____ while at the scene, was, in his opinion, an immediate life-threatening situation, as stated in Section 16.02(i)(1) of the Texas Penal Code.
11. That the interception of _____ (wire/oral) communications was necessary in order to effect a safe termination of the immediate life-threatening situation.
12. That no interception of any wire or oral communications had been done or attempted prior to the telephone call to the magistrate.

13. That, if granted by me, the interception of said communications would begin and continue only until the life-threatening situation has terminated.

BASED UPON THE AFORESAID, and in compliance with Section 16.02(c)(5) of the Texas Penal Code, I granted the request to intercept (wire/oral) communications occurring at _____ Tarrant County, Texas.

On this date, the _____ day of _____, 20_____, personally appeared before me, being the same person referred to earlier in this order. He or she related to me the following:

1. That after receiving my authorization at _____o'clock _____ a.m/p.m. on the _____day of _____, 20_____, the interception of (wire/oral) communications at _____, Tarrant County, Texas was initiated.
2. That the life-threatening situation within the said location was terminated at _____o'clock _____a.m./p.m. on the day of _____, 20_____, and the aforesaid interception terminated at that time.
3. That an effort was made to tape record any interception made.

IT IS HEREBY ORDERED THAT THE ORIGINAL TAPED RECORDINGS OF:

1. My conversation with _____ in which I authorized the aforesaid interception; and
2. Any original recordings of the interception, _____ be safely kept by _____ for a period of not less than 180 days from the date of this order.

It is further ordered that this ORDER be docketed in the official records of this court.

Done and entered this _____day of _____, _____.

Dated this _____day of _____, 20_____
_____

Bibliography

Allen, D.A. (1973). Peer counseling and professional responsibility. *American College Health Association Journal, 21,* 35-40.

American Psychiatric Association (1994). *Diagnostic and statistical manual of mental disorders* (Fourth edition). Washington, DC: American Psychiatric Association.

American Psychiatric Assocation (2001). *Guidelines for teen suicide and intervention.* Washington, DC: American Psychiatric Association.

Anonymous (1997a). Domestic violence injuries soar. *Law Enforcement Technology,* November, 18.

Anonymous (1997b). Domestic violence—police [video segment]. *Dateline,* aired December 14.

Anonymous (1997c). Innovative strategies to reduce the incidence of domestic violence involving police officers. Paper prepared by the International Association of Chiefs of Police. October.

Arieti, S. (1963). Psychopathic personality: Some views on its psychopathology and psychodynamics. *Comprehensive Psychiatry,* October, 7-14.

Aumiller, G.S. and Goldfarb, D.A. (1997). Domestic violence statistics. Presentation given at IACP Convention, Orlando, Florida. October.

Bernstein, R. (1995). A nation learning to kill, and learning to like it. *The New York Times,* October 13, p. 33, section C.

Biggs, J.R. (1987). Defusing hostage situations. *The Police Chief,* May, 33-37.

Blum, L.N. (1987). Officer survival after trauma: The companion officer program. *Journal of California Law Enforcement,* August, 8-11.

Bolz, F. (1979). *Hostage cop.* New York: Rawson, Wade Publishers.

Bolz, F. and Schlossberg, H. (1982). *Hostage Negotiation.* Seminar handout workbook. Huntington Station, NY.

Boyd, L., Carlson, D., Smith, R., and Sykes, G.W. (1995). Domestic assault among police: A survey of internal affairs policies. Advanced management college paper series, Southwestern Law Enforcement Institute of the Southwestern Legal Foundation and the Arlington, Texas Police Department.

Cannon, W.B. (1960 [1932]). *The wisdom of the body.* New York: Norton.

Carkhuff, R.R. and Truax, C. (1969). Lay mental health counseling. *Journal of Consulting Psychology, 29*(5), 5-10.

Carroll, M. (1973). The regeneration of guidance. *The School Counselor, 20*(5), 355-360.

Cicirelli, V.G. (1972). The effect of sibling relationship on concept learning of young children taught by child-teachers. *Child Development, 43,* 282-287.

CONTOMS (1993). Emergency medical technician—tactical [brochure].

Cooper, H.H.A. (1997). Negotiating with terrorists. *The International Journal of Police Negotiations and Crisis Management,* spring, 1-8.

Davis, R.C. (1987). Three prudent considerations for hostage negotiators. *Law and Order,* September, 10-15.

Defina, M.P. and Wetherbee, L. (1997). Advocacy and law enforcement: Partners in domestic violence. *Law Enforcement Bulletin,* October, 12-15.

Dolan, J.T. and Fuselier, G.D. (1989). A guide for first responders to hostage situations. *FBI Law Enforcement Bulletin,* April, 10-15.

Eisdorf, C. and Golann, S.E. (1969). Principles for training of new professionals in mental health. *Community Mental Health Journal, 5,* 349-357.

Engle, K.B. and Szyperski, T.A. (1965). *A demonstration study of significant others in producing changes in self-concept and achievement in Kalamazoo secondary school underachievers.* Kalamazoo, MI: Kalamazoo Board of Education.

Evarts, W.R., Greenstone, J.L., Kirkpatrick, G., and Leviton, S.C. (1984). *Winning through accommodation: The mediator's handbook.* Dubuque: Kendall/Hunt.

FBI Instructional Material (1984, 1994). FBI Academy. Federal Bureau of Investigation, Quantico, VA.

Feltgen, J. (1996). Domestic violence: When the abuser is a police officer. *The Police Chief,* October, 3-7.

Fisher, R., Ury, W., and Patton, B. (1991). Getting to yes. New York: Penguin Books.

Fowler, W.R. (1997). Dealing with defenestrators: Immediate intervention. *International Journal of Police Negotiations and Crisis Management,* spring, 1-10.

Fowler, W.R. and Greenstone, J.L. (1983). Hostage negotiations. In R. Corsini (Ed.), *Encyclopedia of Psychology,* (p. 142). New York: John Wiley and Sons.

Fowler, W.R. and Greenstone, J.L. (1987). Hostage negotiations for police. In R. Corsini (Ed.), *Concise Encyclopedia of Psychology,* (pp. 530-531). New York: John Wiley Interscience.

Fowler, W.R. and Greenstone, J.L. (1989). *Crisis intervention compendium.* Littleton, MA: Copley Publishing Group.

Fowler, W.R. and Greenstone, J.L. (1996). Hostage negotiations for police. In R. Corsini (Ed.), *Concise encyclopedia of psychology,* Second edition (pp. 421-422). New York: Wiley Interscience.

Fuselier, G.W. (1981). A practical overview of hostage negotiations. *FBI Law Enforcement Bulletin,* June/July, 2-5.

Fuselier, G.W. (1986). What every negotiator would like his chief to know. *FBI Law Enforcement Bulletin 55,* 12-15.

Greenstone, J.L. (1978). An interdisciplinary approach to marital disputes arbitration: The Dallas plan. *Conciliation Courts Review,* June, 2-8.

Greenstone, J.L. (1980). Childhood crises. March. Dallas: WFAA Radio.

Greenstone, J.L. (1981a). Crisis intervention: Stress and the police officer. Paper presented to the Society for Police and Criminal Psychology, Baton Rouge, LA. October.

Greenstone, J.L. (1981b). Job-related stress: Is it killing you? *National Law Journal,* Law Office Management Section, December 21, 33-34.

Greenstone, J.L. (1983). The divorce referee. *Dallas Morning News,* Today section, February 13, 2.

Greenstone, J.L. (1984a). The crisis at Christmas. *Emotional First Aid: Journal of Crisis Intervention,* winter, 30-35.

Greenstone, J.L. (1984b). Holiday doesn't replace therapy: Crisis steps to avoid. *Northwest Passage.* Tarrant County Junior College, December 13, 4-8.

Greenstone, J.L. (1986). The laws of terrorism. *Emotional First Aid: A Journal of Crisis Intervention,* winter, 22-25.

Greenstone, J.L. (1989). *A hostage negotiations team training manual for small and medium size police departments.* Dallas: Leviton and Greenstone.

Greenstone, J.L. (1992a). The art of negotiating: Tactics and negotiating techniques—The way of the past and the way of the future. *Command: Journal of the Texas Tactical Police Officers Association, 1,* 5-9.

Greenstone, J.L. (1992b). The key to success for hostage negotiations teams: Training, training and more training. *The Police Forum, 20,* 2-3.

Greenstone, J.L. (1992c). Mediation advocacy: A new concept in the arena of family dispute resolution. Paper presented to the Sixth International Congress of Family Therapy, Jerusalem, Israel, and in *Critical Issues in Crisis Intervention, Hostage Negotiations and Conflict Resolution in the Opening Decades of the Twenty-First Century.* April, 100-111.

Greenstone, J.L. (1992d). The negotiator's equipment: Tools of the trade; mark of the professional. *Law Enforcement Product News, 20,* 1-5.

Greenstone, J.L. (1993a). Crisis intervention skills training for police negotiators in the 21st century. *Command,* summer, 6-11.

Greenstone, J.L. (1993b). *Critical incident stress debriefing and crisis management.* Austin, TX: Texas Department of Health.

Greenstone, J.L. (1993c). *A mediation primer.* Dallas: Leviton and Greenstone.

Greenstone, J.L. (1993d). Violence in the courtroom: Culpability, personal responsibility, sensitivity and justice including the courtroom violence risk analysis.

Greenstone, J.L. (1993e). Violence in the courtroom: Culpability, personal responsibility, sensitivity and justice—The courtroom risk analysis checklist. *National Social Science Perspectives Journal: Proceedings of the November 1993 National Social Science Association San Antonio Conference, 4*(1), 15-36. San Antonio, Texas: National Social Science Association.

Greenstone, J.L. (1993f). Violence in the courtroom, part one. *Texas Police Journal,* October, 17-19.

Greenstone, J.L. (1993g). Violence in the courtroom, part two. *Texas Police Journal,* November, 15-18.

Greenstone, J.L. (1995a). Crisis intervention skills training for negotiators. *The Police Chief,* August, 14-19.

Greenstone, J.L. (1995b). Hostage negotiations team training for small police departments. In Martin I. Kurke and Ellen M. Scrivner (Eds.), *Police Psychology into the 21st Century* (pp. 279-296). Hillsdale, NJ: Lawrence Erlbaum Associates.

Greenstone, J.L. (1995c). Police crisis negotiations with AIDS patients and HTLV III/HIV positive persons. *The Journal of Crisis Negotiations,* fall, 10-16.

Greenstone, J.L. (1995d). Tactics and negotiating techniques (TNT): The way of the past and the way of the future. In Martin I. Kurke and Ellen M. Scrivner (Eds.), *Police psychology into the 21st century* (pp. 357-371). Hillsdale, NJ: Lawrence Erlbaum Associates.

Greenstone, J.L. (1997). Krisenintervention: mitteilungen (Crisis intervention communications in hostage and crisis negotiations). Paper and presentation to the Internationale Seminar-Fuhrung, Einsatz, Ausbildung und Ausstaattung von Specialeinheiten, Polizei-Fuhrungsakademie, Munster, Germany. August.

Greenstone, J.L. (1998a). Basic course for hostage and crisis negotiators. Arlington, TX: Regional Police Academy, North Central Texas Council of Governments.

Greenstone, J.L. (1998b). Domestic violence. *Signal 50,* Fort Worth Police Officers Association, January, 3-4.

Greenstone, J.L. (1998c). Domestic violence II: Signals of violence and murder. *Signal 50,* Fort Worth Police Officers Association, February, 7-8.

Greenstone, J.L. (1998d). The role of tactical emergency medical support in hostage and crisis negotiations. *Prehospital and Disaster Medicine,* April-December, 20-28.

Greenstone, J.L. (1999). Elements of hostage and crisis negotiations. Unpublished manuscript.

Greenstone, J.L. (2000a). *Online course in basic hostage and crisis negotiations.* Minneapolis: Walden University.

Greenstone, J.L. (2000b). Peer support in a municipal police department. *The Forensic Examiner,* March/April, 10-15.

Greenstone, J.L. (2001a). Case study: Why did it work? *Journal of Police Crisis Negotiations,* fall, 127-130.

Greenstone, J.L. (2001b). Fit to serve: Failure to address stress can cause emotional problems. *Civil Air Patrol News,* March, 10.

Greenstone, J.L. (2001c). Fit to serve: Holiday stress—some steps to help you avoid a crisis at Christmas. *Civil Air Patrol News,* November, 10.

Greenstone, J.L. (2001d). Fit to serve: Teen suicide. *Civil Air Patrol News,* September, 11.

Greenstone, J.L. (2001e). New initiatives: The role of tactical emergency medical support in hostage and crisis negotiations. *Journal of Police Crisis Negotiations,* fall, 29-33.

Greenstone, J.L. (2001f). Terrorism and our response to it: The new normalcy. *Signal 50,* Fort Worth Police Officers Association, November, 34-35.

Greenstone, J.L. (2002a). Fit to serve: The drugs of abuse. *Civil Air Patrol News,* May, 7.

Greenstone, J.L. (2002b). Fit to serve: Terrorism and our response: Getting on with our life and our mission. *Civil Air Patrol News,* February, 10, 19.

Greenstone, J.L. (2003a). Case study: How to be a mental health consultant. *Journal of Police Crisis Negotiations,* spring, 121-130.

Greenstone, J.L. (2003b). Crisis and hostage negotiations: Six steps to the training and performance of police negotiators. *Journal of Police Crisis Negotiations,* spring, 51-58.

Greenstone, J.L., Dunn, J.M., and Leviton, S.C. (1994). Promotion of mental health for police: The departmental peer counselling programme. In D.R. Trent and C.A. Reed (Eds.), *Promotion of Mental Health,* Volume 4 (pp. 319-340). Aldershot, Hants, England: Avebury, Ashgate Publishing Limited.

Greenstone, J.L., Dunn, J.M., and Leviton, S. (1995). Police peer counseling and crisis intervention services into the 21st century: Crisis intervention, Volume 2. (Presentations based on this paper were given in London, Northern Ireland–Queens College, and University of Southampton, England.)

Greenstone, J.L., Kosson, D.S., and Gacono, C.B. (2000). Psychopathy and hostage negotiations: Some preliminary thoughts and findings. In Carl B. Gacono (Ed.), *The clinical and forensic assessment of psychopathy: A practitioner's guide* (pp. 385-404). Hillsdale, NJ: Lawrence Erlbaum Associates.

Greenstone, J.L. and Leviton, S. (1979a). *The crisis intervener's handbook,* Volume 1. Dallas: Crisis Management Workshops.

Greenstone, J.L. and Leviton, S. (1979b). Crisis intervention. *P.M. Magazine.* September. Dallas: WFAA Television.

Greenstone, J.L. and Leviton, S. (1979c). *Crisis management and intervener survival.* Tulsa: Affective House.

Greenstone, J.L. and Leviton, S. (1979d). Intervention and emergency therapy in marriage and family crises. Paper presented to the Third International Congress of Family Therapy and Family Life Education, Tel Aviv, Israel. July.

Greenstone, J.L. and Leviton, S. (1979e). *Stress reduction: Personal energy management.* Tulsa: Affective House.

Greenstone, J.L. and Leviton, S. (1980-1987). Crisis intervention in mediation. Training presentation to Mediator Training Courses, Dispute Mediation Service of Dallas, Texas.

Greenstone, J.L. and Leviton, S. (1980a). *The crisis interveners handbook,* Volume II. Dallas: Rothschild Publishing House.

Greenstone, J.L. and Leviton, S. (1980b). Crisis management: A basic concern. *Crisis Interveners Newsletter,* January, 1-2.

Greenstone, J.L. and Leviton, S. (1981a). Crisis management and intervener survival. In Raymond Corsini (Ed.), *Innovative psychotherapies* (pp. 249-250). New York: John Wiley Interscience.

Greenstone, J.L. and Leviton, S. (1981b). *Hotline: Crisis intervention directory.* New York: Facts on File.

Greenstone, J.L. and Leviton, S. (1981c). *Training the trainer.* Tulsa: Affective House.

Greenstone, J.L. and Leviton, S. (1982). *Crisis intervention: Handbook for interveners.* Dubuque: Kendall-Hunt.

Greenstone, J.L. and Leviton, S. (1983a). Crisis intervention. In Raymond Corsini (Ed.), *Encyclopedia of Psychology* (pp. 312-315). New York: John Wiley and Sons.

Greenstone, J.L. and Leviton, S. (1983b). Divorce mediation. *D Magazine, Inside Dallas.* January, 20-22.

Greenstone, J.L. and Leviton, S. (1983c). Divorce mediation and the attorney. Dallas Bar Association, Dallas, Texas. March.

Greenstone, J.L. and Leviton, S. (1983d). Executive survival. In Raymond Corsini (Ed.), *Encyclopedia of Psychology* (pp. 249-250). New York: John Wiley and Sons.

Greenstone, J.L. and Leviton, S. (1983e). Mediation: An alternative to litigation. Paper presented to the Academy of Criminal Justice Sciences, San Antonio, Texas. March.

Greenstone, J.L. and Leviton, S. (1983f). Mediation: Family dispute resolution. Paper presented to the Fourth International Congress of Family Therapy. Tel Aviv, Israel. July.

Greenstone, J.L. and Leviton, S. (1984a). Crisis intervention in mediation. Paper presented to the National Conference on Peace and Conflict Resolution, St. Louis, Missouri. September.

Greenstone, J.L. and Leviton, S. (1984b). Crisis management for the mediator. Paper and workshop presented to the Second Annual Conference on Problem Solving Through Mediation, Albany, New York. December.

Greenstone, J.L. and Leviton, S. (1984c). Management mediation: The police officer's alternative to litigation. Paper presented to the First National Symposium on Police Psychological Services, Federal Bureau of Investigation Academy, Quantico, Virginia. September.

Greenstone, J.L. and Leviton, S. (1984d). Mediation. Workshop presented to the Family Law Class, Southern Methodist University, Dallas, Texas. October.

Greenstone, J.L. and Leviton, S. (1986a). Alternatives in dispute resolution: Family and marital mediation. Paper presented to the Fifth International Congress of Family Therapy, Jerusalem, Israel. June.

Greenstone, J.L. and Leviton, S. (1986b). Crisis intervention: The emerging discipline—Current issues and practical concerns. Paper presented to the Fifth International Congress of Family Therapy, Jerusalem, Israel. June.

Greenstone, J.L. and Leviton, S. (1986c). The dispute mediator as a crisis manager: Crisis intervention skills for the mediator in high stress, high risk situations. Paper and workshop presented to the Academy of Family Mediators, Minneapolis, Minnesota. July 16-19.

Greenstone, J.L. and Leviton, S. (1986d). Emergency intervention in marriage and family crises. Paper presented to the Fifth International Congress of Family Therapy, Jerusalem, Israel. June.

Greenstone, J.L. and Leviton, S. (1986e). Family dispute mediation. Paper presented to the Texas Council on Family Relations, Arlington, Texas. April.

Greenstone, J.L. and Leviton, S. (1986f). Intervention procedures. *Emotional First Aid: A Journal of Crisis Intervention,* fall, 2-8.

Greenstone, J.L. and Leviton, S. (1986g). Mediation: The police officer's alternative to litigation. Psychological Services for Law Enforcement. Washington, DC: U.S. Department of Justice, Federal Bureau of Investigation, U.S. Government Printing Office, 50-61. December.

Greenstone, J.L. and Leviton, S. (1986h). Referrals: A key to successful crisis intervention. *Emotional First Aid: A Journal of Crisis Intervention,* summer, 18-23.

Greenstone, J.L. and Leviton, S. (1987a). Crisis intervention. In Raymond Corsini (Ed.), *Concise Encyclopedia of Psychology* (pp. 269-270). New York: John Wiley Interscience.

Greenstone, J.L. and Leviton, S. (1987b). Crisis intervention for mediators in high risk, high stress, potentially violent situations. Paper and workshop presented to the Academy of Family Mediators, New York, New York. July.

Greenstone, J.L. and Leviton, S. (1987c). Crisis management for mediators in high stress, high risk, potentially violent situations. *Mediation Quarterly,* September, 25-35.

Greenstone, J.L. and Leviton, S. (1987d). Executive survival. In Raymond Corsini (Ed.), *Concise Encyclopedia of Psychology* (p. 618). New York: John Wiley Interscience.

Greenstone, J.L. and Leviton, S. (1991a). *Parents, kids and war: Brochure of information to assist parents and children in handling war and its consequences.* Dallas and New York: National Broadcasting Company and Columbia Broadcasting System.

Greenstone, J.L. and Leviton, S.C. (1991b). *War, and how to respond to it.* Dallas: Leviton and Greenstone.

Greenstone, J.L. and Leviton, S. (1992). Crisis management for mediators in high stress, high risk potentially violent family and divorce mediations. Paper presented to the Sixth International Congress of Family Therapy, Jerusalem, Israel. April.

Greenstone, J.L. and Leviton, S. (1993). *Elements of crisis intervention.* Pacific Grove, CA: Brooks/Cole.

Greenstone, J.L. and Leviton, S.C. (1996). Crisis intervention. In Raymond Corsini (Ed.), *Concise encyclopedia of psychology* (pp. 209-210), Second edition. New York: John Wiley Interscience.

Greenstone, J.L. and Leviton, S. (2001a). *Parents, kids and war: Information to assist parents and children in handling war and its consequences,* Second edition [booklet]. Fort Worth, Texas: Leviton and Greenstone.

Greenstone, J.L. and Leviton, S. (2001b). Parents, kids, war and our mission. [A brochure to be used by Civil Air Patrol personnel, counselors, critical incident team members, parents, and cadets in an attempt to minimize the psychological trauma resulting from terrorism and war.] Fort Worth, TX: Leviton and Greenstone.

Greenstone, J.L. and Leviton, S. (2002). *Elements of crisis intervention,* Second edition. Pacific Grove, CA: Brooks/Cole.

Greenstone, J.L. and Reich, V. (1972). *Training manual for Truth House counselors with behavioral objectives.* Carrollton-Farmers Branch, TX: Truth House.

Greenstone, J.L. and Rosenbluh, E.S. (1980). Evolution of the American Academy of Crisis Interveners and the Southwestern Academy of Crisis Interveners. *Crisis Interveners Newsletter,* December, 1-3.

Grossman, D. (1995). *The psychological cost of learning to kill in war and society.* New York: Little, Brown and Company.

Gumaer, J. (1976). Training peer facilitators. *Elementary School Guidance and Counseling, 11,* 26-36.

Hamburg, B.A. and Varenhorst, B.B. (1972). Peer counseling in the secondary schools: A community mental health project for youth. *American Journal of Orthopsychiatry, 42*(4), 566-581.

Hare, R.D. (1995). Psychopaths: New trends and research. *The Harvard Mental Health Newsletter,* September, 1-5.

Hendricks, J. and Greenstone, J.L. (1982). Crisis intervention and criminal justice. Paper presented to the Academy of Criminal Justice Sciences, Louisville, Kentucky. March.

Hillmann, M. (1988). Tactical intelligence operations and support during a major barricade/hostage event. *The Police Chief,* February, 20-26.

International Association of Chiefs of Police (1995). Combating workplace violence: Guidelines for employers and law enforcement. Paper prepared by the International Association of Chiefs of Police.

Kosson, D.S. (1997). *Notes for using the interpersonal measures of psychopathy.* November. Unpublished manuscript.

Kosson, D.S., Steuerwald, B.L., Forth, A.E., and Kirkhart, K.J. (1997). A new method for assessing the interpersonal behavior of psychopaths: Preliminary validation studies. *Psychological Assessment, 9,* 89-101.

Lanceley, F.J. (1981). The antisocial personality as a hostage taker. *Journal of Police Science and Administration,* March, 30-40.

Leviton, S.C. and Greenstone, J.L. (1980). Intervener survival: Dealing with the givens. *Emotional First Aid: A Journal of Crisis Intervention, 2,* 15-20.

Leviton, S.C. and Greenstone, J.L. (1983a). Conflict mediation. In Raymond Corsini (Ed.), *Encyclopedia of Psychology* (pp. 270-272). New York: John Wiley and Sons.

Leviton, S.C. and Greenstone, J.L. (1983b). Intervener survival. In Raymond Corsini (Ed.), *Encyclopedia of Psychology* (pp. 249-250). New York: John Wiley and Sons.

Leviton, S.C. and Greenstone, J.L. (1984a). Team intervention. *Emotional First Aid: A Journal of Crisis Intervention, 1,* 20-25.

Leviton, S. and Greenstone, J.L. (1984b). Mediation in potential crisis situations. *Emotional First Aid: A Journal of Crisis Intervention,* winter, 15-26.

Leviton, S.C. and Greenstone, J.L. (1987a). Conflict mediation. In Raymond Corsini (Ed.), *Concise Encyclopedia of Psychology* (pp. 234-236). New York: John Wiley Interscience.

Leviton, S.C. and Greenstone, J.L. (1987b). Intervener survival. In Raymond Corsini (Ed.), *Concise Encyclopedia of Psychology* (p. 618). New York: John Wiley Interscience.

Leviton, S.C. and Greenstone, J.L. (1997). *Elements of mediation.* Pacific Grove, CA: Brooks/Cole.

Leviton, S.C. and Greenstone, J.L. (2002). The hostage and crisis negotiator's training laboratory. *Journal of Police Crisis Negotiations,* fall, 21-33.

McMains, M.J. and Lanceley, F.J. (1995). The use of crisis intervention principles by police negotiators. *The Journal of Crisis Negotiations,* fall, 25-28.

McMains, M.J. and Mullins, W.C. (1996). *Crisis negotiations: Managing critical incidents and hostage situations in law enforcement and corrections.* Cincinnati: Anderson Publishing Company.

Mitchell, D. and Hare, R.D. (1996). Psychopathy and unlawful confinement: Delving into the psyche of the hostage taker. Unpublished paper.

Mitchell, J.T. and Resnik, H.L.P. (1981). *Emergency response to crisis.* Bowie, MD: Robert J. Brady Company.

Mordock, J.B., Ellis, M.H., and Greenstone, J.L. (1969). The effects of group and individual therapy on sociometric choice of disturbed adolescents. *International Journal of Group Psychotherapy, 4,* 200-210.

Pederson, P.A. (1988). *A handbook for developing multicultural awareness.* New York: American Association for Counseling and Development.

Rosenbluh, E.S. (1986). *Crisis counseling: Emotional first aid.* Dubuque: Kendall/ Hunt.

Ryan, A.H. (1997). Afterburn: The victimization of police families. *The Police Chief,* October, 20-25.

Sadusky, J. (1997). *Working effectively with the police: A guide for battered women's advocates.* Battered Women's Justice Project, Minneapolis, Minnesota. October.

Sewell, J.D. (1983). Police stress. *FBI Law Enforcement Bulletin,* April, 10-12.

Slaikeu, K.A. (1984). *Crisis intervention: A handbook for practice and research.* Boston: Allyn and Bacon.

Soskis, D.A. and Van Zandt, C.R. (1986). Hostage negotiations: Law enforcement's most effective non-lethal weapon. *FBI Management Quarterly,* fall, 15-21.

Stelle, E.J. (1974). *The traumatic incident corps.* The City of Portland, Oregon: Bureau of Police.

Strentz, T. (1979). Law enforcement policy and ego defenses of the hostage. *FBI Law Enforcement Bulletin,* April, 10-13.

Strentz, T. (1983). The inadequate personality as a hostage taker. *Journal of Police Science and Administration,* March, 30-35.

U.S. Department of Justice, Federal Bureau of Investigation (2003). *Uniform crime report: Law enforcement officers killed and assaulted, 1990-1993.* Washington, DC: U.S. Government Printing Office.

Vriend, T.J. (1969). High performing: Inner-city adolescents assist lower performing peers in counseling groups. *Personnel and Guidance Journal, 47*(9), 847-904.

Wesselius, C.L. (1983). The anatomy of a hostage situation. *Behavioral Sciences and the Law, 1*(2), 10-15.

Index

Page numbers followed by the letter "b" indicate boxed text; those followed by the letter "f" indicate figures; and those followed by the letter "t" indicate tables.

ELEMENTS OF NEGOTIATIONS BY TOPIC